G000125575

Shrines of Ireland

John J. Dunne

Shrines of Ireland

First published 1989 by
Veritas Publications
7/8 Lower Abbey Street
Dublin 1

Copyright © John J. Dunne 1989

ISBN 1 85390 028 I

The publishers are grateful to the following for permission to reproduce their
copyright material: Bord Fáilte for photographs on pages 14(top), 18, 22, 33,
36, 38, 68, 77, 84, 91, 94, 128, 131, 134 and 141; the Commissioners of Public
Works for photographs on pages 30, 49, 65, 74, 125 and 137(top) and to the
following for supplying photographs: Frank Gavin Ltd; Photography, Dublin
(pages 55, 59(bottom), 98, 102, 110, 113, 117, 121;*The Drogheda Independent*
(page 107); Tomás Hayes, Wexford (page 105); Don MacMonagle, Killarney
(page 52); Redmonds, Roscrea (page 45); *The Limerick Leader* (page 26); Rev.
Sean Walsh, IC, PP, Faughart (page 71); The Church of Ireland Press Office,
Belfast (page 14);Rev. John McCarthy, CC, Claddaghduff, Co. Galway (page
137, bottom); Rev. Athanasius O'Brien, OCSO, Mount Melleray (page 42) and
Intercom, 4 Dublin Road, Stillorgan, Co. Dublin (pages 59(top), 60, 81); Dublin
County Council (page 87).

Cover design by David Cooke
Typesetting by Printset and Design Ltd, Dublin
Printed in the Republic of Ireland by Mount Salus Press Ltd, Dublin 8.

Contents

Foreword 9
Introduction 11

Ulster
Armagh 13
Lough Derg 17

Munster
Ardmore 21
Bishop O'Brien Memorial Chapel 25
Cashel 29
Glenstal Abbey 32
St Finbarr's Hollow 35
Holy Cross Abbey 37
Mount Melleray 40
Mount St Joseph's 44
Skellig Michael 48
St Mary's Cathedral, Killarney 51

Leinster
Tomb of Paul Cullen 54
Cathedrals of Dublin 58
Church of the Most Holy Trinity 64
Clonmacnois 67
Shrine of St Brigid, Faughart 70
Fore 73
Glendalough 76
Irish Lourdes 79
Jerpoint Abbey 83
Madonna of Malahide 86
Mellifont Abbey 90
Monasterboice 93
Mother Mary Aikenhead Shrine 97
Our Lady of Dublin 101

Our Lady's Island 104
Shrine of St Oliver Plunkett 106
Shrine of St Valentine 109
Tomb of Father Charles 112
Tomb of Father John Sullivan 116
Tomb of Matt Talbot 120

Connacht
Ballintubber Abbey 124
Croagh Patrick 127
Knock 130
Kylemore Abbey 133
The church they dug from the sands, Omey Island.. 136
Sligo Abbey 140

*To the memory of
my mother*

Foreword

If the title of this book implies totality, no presumption is intended. It would be a monumental task, indeed, to list, let alone detail, all the shrines of Ireland. Let the term embrace churches, altars, tombs, statues and all those casual artefacts created to preserve a memory, from wall tablets to wayside crosses, and you have a vast field that never can be fully plumbed. They are as plentiful as fraughans on the slopes of the Knockmealdowns.

The ruined abbey outside the village, the crumbling church tower in the forgotten corner of a demesne, the holy well with its sad little shreds of cloth clinging to surrounding bushes, the lonely plaque on the back road where in troubled times a young man was shot dead, the small crossroads crucifix where another lost his life in a motor-cycle accident: all these are the shrines of Ireland.

There are the great shrines: Holy Cross, Monasterboice, Clonmacnois, Ballintubber. There are the sad shrines: the tomb of humble Matt Talbot, the bones of martyred St Valentine, the cruelly severed head of St Oliver Plunkett at Drogheda. There are the indomitable, indestructible shrines: Skellig Michael, Cashel, the sand-covered church of Omey.

All are crocheted together, woven into the fabric of Christian Ireland through the centuries, so that even the most primitive beehive cell on an Atlantic-washed island shares common purpose with the cathedral spire, and both are mirrored in the rainwater that has rested in the Deer Stone at Glendalough.

John J. Dunne
Dublin

Acknowledgements

I wish to acknowledge the help and courtesy I have received from the following in the preparation of this book: The officials and staffs of Dublin University, the National University of Ireland, the National Library of Ireland, the Central Catholic Library, Bord Fáilte Éireann (Irish Tourist Board), the Northern Ireland Tourist Board, the Royal Irish Academy and the Old Dublin Society. I am also grateful to the numerous other sources and individuals consulted.

A special word of thanks is due to Dr Brendan Comiskey, Bishop of Ferns, and to Mr Nick Lundberg, Editor of *The Irish Catholic*.

Introduction

'The ruined abbey outside the village, the crumbling church tower in the forgotten corner of a demesne, the holy well with its sad little shreds of cloth clinging to surrounding bushes, the lonely plaque on the back road where in troubled times a young man was shot dead, the small crossroads crucifix where another lost his life in a motorcycle accident: all these are the shrines of Ireland'.

Indeed they are, and John J. Dunne captures the main features of many of them as he flashes them before us in a series of literary snapshots. Some are well known, for example Knock, Lough Derg and Clonmacnois. Some are not so well known, except perhaps at local level, for example the Bishop O'Brien Memorial Chapel in Limerick, the Madonna of Malahide and Paul Cullen's tomb in Clonliffe College.

All are filled with memories of the giants of history, the heroes and heroines of the faith, their artefacts, and other accomplishments they have left behind to add to the magic and mystique of Ireland. It is good for us to remember them, to walk their land and our land, to visit their resting places, to pray in their chapels, to gaze in awe at their masterpieces. The author helps us find our roots, to stand on the shoulders of those who are part of the story we continue to write on the face of our lovely land.

In an age of rapid change, it is good to pause and remember and hope. This book presents us with the 'where' of remembering and the 'why' of hoping.

✠ BRENDAN COMISKEY
Bishop of Ferns

Bishop's House,
Wexford.

Armagh

The cathedrals on the hills

There is a charming story that is part of the folklore of Armagh. It tells us that while St Patrick and the local king, Daire, were walking with their attendants in the valley between the two adjoining hills upon which the cathedrals of Armagh stand today, they came upon a doe with her fawn.

The attendants were about to kill both animals when St Patrick intervened and stopped them. Then, placing the fawn on his shoulders, with the doe following, he carried it to the hill on which the Catholic cathedral was to be built centuries later and let it loose in the thick woods that then covered the hill.

St Patrick had come to Armagh in that year (443) to establish his primatial see on the hill called Ard Macha, granted to him for the purpose by King Daire. Although the king at first restricted Patrick's activities to the lower slopes of the hill, he later repented and allowed the Christian settlement to extend.

Armagh, even then, had a historic past. As far back as 300 BC the warrior queen Macha established her great fort, Eamhain Macha, as her royal residence west of the site of the subsequent town centre.

When the fame of St Patrick's monastic school there spread, Armagh became a great centre of learning, attracting students from many faraway places.

It was still a flourishing settlement, important enough to warrant a visit from the High King of Ireland, when Brian Boru arrived and remained for a week in 1004. During his visit, the city officials paid him great honour, solemnly placing in his hands their famous Book of Armagh and, within it, duly recording his visit. Brian, in turn, presented

Armagh's two cathedrals — the Catholic (above) and Church of Ireland (below)

the city with twenty ounces of gold. A decade later Brian was to return to Armagh, this time to be buried there, after his death at the battle of Clontarf.

Between 1014, the year of Brian's death, and the Anglo-Norman invasion of 1169, Armagh passed through a period of brilliance. In 1169 another High King came in the majestic person of Ruairi O'Connor, the last High King of Ireland. There, O'Connor founded a professorship 'for all the Irish and the Scots'.

Armagh was to suffer attacks by the Norse and many humiliations, and more than once over the centuries it was to be destroyed and then raised again from the rubble. In 1566 Shane O'Neill's Irish forces laid waste to the town to prevent its occupation by the English. In 1642 Armagh was again destroyed by another O'Neill, Phelim.

Imposingly situated on its hilltop, the Catholic cathedral is approached by an impressive series of steps set out in attractive terraces. Erected between the years 1840 and 1873 in decorated Gothic style, it has a splendid west front surmounted by tall twin spires. Inside the walls are richly decorated with a generous splash of mosaic and marble and medallions depicting the saints of Ireland. High overhead hang the red hats of some of the Cardinal Archbishops of Armagh of the past.

The cathedral adjoins Ara Coeli, the residence of the Archbishop, while close at hand is the Diocesan College of St Patrick.

Armagh's Protestant cathedral also stands imposingly on its own hill, on the traditional site of the church built by St Patrick. It is a well-proportioned structure in perpendicular Gothic fashion with a low, battlemented tower rising from the intersection of the nave and transepts. The cathedral as it stands today is mainly the product of an accumulation of eighteenth- and nineteenth-century restorations.

The cathedral contains several interesting monuments, among them a statue by Roubiliac of St Thomas Molyneaux (1661-1733) and some effigies of former Archbishops of

Armagh, while the north transept, now the vestry, contains evocative seventeenth-century memorials of the Caulfield family, the Earls of Charlemont.

Outside the north transept of the cathedral there is a tablet reputed to mark the site of Brian Boru's grave.

The Palace, the official residence of the Protestant Archbishop, which was built for Archbishop Robinson, is approached through its own demesne from Dublin Street. It has an attractive chapel designed by Francis Johnston and Thomas Coolly while in the demesne itself are the ruins of a Franciscan friary dating from 1266.

As well as having a hand in designing the chapel of the Archbishop's Palace, Francis Johnston, who was born in the town, designed Armagh's courthouse.

Other interesting focal points for the visitor are the Royal School, founded by Charles I in 1627, the Observatory, established by Archbishop Robinson in 1791, and the excellent County Museum.

In Ogle Street there is a tablet over a shop thought to be the traditional birthplace of St Malachy, who died in the arms of the great St Bernard at Clairvaux in 1148.

The Book of Armagh, which figured in the visit of Brian Boru to Armagh in 1004, happily has survived the centuries. Today it may be seen in the Library of Trinity College in Dublin. It consists of the New Testament in Latin, with the Confession of St Patrick, two lives of St Patrick, together with other pieces of writing transcribed by the hand of the scribe Ferdomnach in 807.

Lough Derg

St Patrick's Purgatory, County Donegal

It was known as the red lake and legend maintained that on the three-acre island there, a dark, lonesome cave was, in fact, the entrance to Purgatory. Strange visions could be seen there and people standing at its grim entrance could speak to the dead.

Such old stories, it seems, had their source in the visit to the island of a young soldier, Knight Owen, who came on pilgrimage in the middle of the twelfth century and who witnessed some strange occurrences in the cave. It was said, too, that Dante's *Divine Comedy* was influenced by the legends of Lough Derg.

Lough Derg is set in the heart of barren Donegal moorland, about four miles from the village of Pettigo on the Donegal-Fermanagh border. Here, it is said, with very little historical probability, St Patrick spent forty days in fasting and prayer. Today its six penitential beds testify to the tiny island on the lake being a place of pilgrimage as far back as the eighth century. It was mentioned as such in the Annals of Ireland in 784 and attracted many pilgrims from continental Europe in the Middle Ages.

It was at Lough Derg that the Prince of Breifne, Tiernan O'Rourke, was on pilgrimage in 1152 when his wife eloped. Its fame spread as far as Sienna, where St Catherine heard about the distant penitential island in Ireland.

Turlough O'Carolan, the blind bard, it was said, met an old love here. She had been his first love and he recognised her by the touch of her hand, although they had been parted for more than twenty years and both had married. As she helped the bard into the island boat, he suddenly cried out: 'This is the hand of Bridget Cruise!'

From the twelfth to the fifteenth century, noblemen from many of the royal houses of Europe made the hazardous

Lough Derg, just before the newest building was erected

journey to County Donegal to follow the prescribed spiritual exercises. These consisted of pilgrims being locked up in the cave for twenty-four hours, representing time spent in Purgatory. Today the huge doors of the basilica on Lough Derg are closed each evening to represent imprisonment for a time before resurrection.

In the fifteenth century, the duration of the Lough Derg pilgrimage was reduced from fifteen to nine days. Pilgrims then ate only bread and water once a day and starved themselves completely on the day before they kept vigil in the cave. When they emerged, they were obliged to plunge three times into the lake as a symbol of being cleansed.

In 1497, opposition to Lough Derg and its pilgrim practices came from Pope Alexander VI who forbade the faithful to go there. Despite this, pilgrims continued to arrive from all over Europe. A few years later, in 1503, a Papal Bull not only cancelled the ban but granted wide indulgences to all who made the pilgrimage. In 1522 the legend of Lough Derg found a place in the Roman Missal.

Opposition was renewed in 1632 when the Reformation

brought a Government order banning it as a place of pilgrimage. Soldiers were placed on guard to ensure that this edict was observed and all the stones and relics associated with St Patrick and the early saints were smashed.

At that time, Queen Henrietta Maria, the Catholic wife of Charles I, appealed to have the lake island restored as a place of pilgrimage, but her pleas were ignored. However, despite the ban, pilgrims persisted in coming to the island and eventually the prohibition was relaxed and the guards withdrawn.

In 1704, by an Act of Queen Anne, all those landing on the island were fined ten shillings or, in default, were publicly whipped by soldiers. Nevertheless, a few years later, the Bishop of Clogher was reporting to Rome that many thousands of pilgrims of all ages were finding their way there to fast and pray.

In the cruel famine year of 1846 no fewer than 30,000 pilgrims wended their way to Lough Derg, an indication of the influence and reputation of the place.

The Basilica of St Patrick on the island was consecrated in May 1931 by Cardinal MacRory, Archbishop of Armagh, and raised to the status of Minor Basilica by Pope Pius XI. Today the basilica is noted for its fine stained-glass windows by the celebrated Harry Clarke of Dublin. These depict Our Lady, St Paul and the Apostles, each carrying one of the Stations of the Cross. The smaller, older church, dedicated to Our Lady, dates from 1870.

The pilgrim season at Lough Derg opens on 1 June and closes on 15 August. The nearest mainland village is Pettigo and from a jetty there a ferry takes pilgrims across Lough Derg to the island. There is an organised three-day programme of prayer and penance. Pilgrims fast from the midnight before their arrival on the island, which must be before 3.00 p.m. They are restricted to one meal each day, consisting of black tea and dry bread or oatcake.

The first night is passed in vigil and there is a strict rule of silence all the time. Most of the routine is spent following the Stations of the Cross and in prayer before the shrines of St Patrick and St Brigid. The prescribed prayers on the island are the repetition of the Our Father, Hail Mary and the Creed.

Full information is always available from the Prior, Lough Derg, Pettigo, County Donegal, Ireland.

Ardmore

Monastic centre of St Declan, County Waterford

In this seventh-century settlement on Ardmore Bay, with its long beach and extensive ecclesiastical remains, founded by St Declan, the pilgrim finds St Declan's oratory, called locally, in Irish, an beannachán, or the little peaked building. In the south-east corner of this building, tradition tells us, the saint is buried. There is the cathedral, built in various stages between the tenth and fourteenth centuries, a 95ft round tower, one of the most perfectly preserved in Ireland, and Temple Disert, the Hermitage Church. Close by is St Declan's holy well and, on the beach beneath the village, a glacial boulder known as St Declan's stone.

The stone is poised on top of outcrop rocks on the seashore, in such a position that the visitor can creep beneath it. It is said locally that to pass beneath the stone is to enjoy a relief from all rheumatic complaints, provided the pilgrim is in the state of grace.

Local lore at Ardmore holds that Declan was the son of a chieftain named Erc, of the noble tribe of the Déise. These people originally came from Meath, where they owned a large expanse of land known as Déise Teamhrach. One of the clan's chiefs, Aengus, having been conquered by King Cormac in a quarrel about the succession to the position of High King of Ireland, left Meath with his followers at the end of the third century and settled in County Waterford. He named his new territory Déise Deisceart, or South Decies, in honour of his original home.

The cathedral is an interesting mixture of features of various styles and periods ranging over several centuries. The nave and chancel are divided by an outstanding pointed arch supported by beautiful semi-columns set off with sculptured capitals. On the north wall of the building is a

Round tower and ruined church at Ardmore, County Waterford

series of panels that were probably originally filled with appropriate frescoes.

There are fifteenth-century altar-tombs on each side wall of the nave, while an interesting opening in the north wall of the chancel leads to a passage within the thick wall. There are two ogham stones, one of which carries a long inscription.

The most remarkable feature of the cathedral at Ardmore, however, is the external arcading of the west gable. This consists of two rows (one above the other) of round-headed panels filled with sculptured scenes. Depicted here are such scriptural subjects as Adam and Eve, the judgment of Solomon, the adoration of the Magi and the Archangel Michael weighing souls. One panel shows the conversion of the pagan prince of the Déise, who ruled over this part of County Waterford.

One of the most memorable features of Ardmore is its splendidly preserved round tower. Measuring 95ft in height and 15ft in diameter at its base, it is one of the most perfect of its kind in Ireland.

Although the tower at Ardmore probably dates from the twelfth century, such round towers were first constructed in the ninth century as a defence against Viking raids. Treasures belonging to the monastery could be stored in them when the settlement was under attack and monks could retreat into them to escape the raiders. Like all similar round towers, the entrance to the tower at Ardmore is high above the ground. Monks could reach this with the aid of a ladder, which they could then draw up into the tower after them.

St Declan's parents were pagan but when they were converted to Christianity by an early Christian missionary, this holy man baptised Declan and foretold his future fame. He was reared by a kinsman named Dobran until he was seven years old and then placed in the charge of a renowned Christian teacher named Dymna. By the time he reached manhood he had a widespread reputation for sanctity and attracted many disciples. Having been ordained in Rome, he returned to Ireland and to Ardmore where he established a church and monastery and became its first bishop.

A legend attached to St Declan's stone stems from the end of his sojourn in Italy:

'When the saint was returning to Ireland from Rome he left behind the bells for the church which he intended to erect here. Early on the morning following his arrival he stood upon the cliff looking out to sea. Suddenly, up from the waters came a silvery sound of chiming and the large black stone came sailing into the bay, bearing upon it the forgotten bells, which invisible angelic hands had set ringing to greet the man of God'.

An old record paints a description of the saint of Ardmore: 'He was handsome in person; in birth and rank, noble; humble in dress and demeanour, sweet in eloquence, great in counsel; energetic in discourse, abounding in charity, cheerful in behaviour, in life holy, in wonders and miracles frequent and renowned.'

St Patrick appointed Declan bishop over the Déise in 449. He died the following year and from then until the beginning of the thirteenth century Ardmore continued to be an Episcopal See. St Ultan was Declan's successor.

From known records of the monastery founded by St Declan, it seems to have been of particular rule, but later it became a house of the Canons Regular of St Augustine. The Annals of Munster tell us that in AD 1174 its abbot, Eugene, was a subscribing witness to the charter granted to the monastery of St Finbarr in Cork.

Bishop O'Brien Memorial Chapel

St Saviour's, Glentworth Street, Limerick

In Limerick city today there is a tranquil spot somewhere on the ancient hill of Cluain, close to the Good Shepherd Convent, unmarked and silent now, but once the setting for the last terrible moments of a martyr's finest hour. There was shouting that day from the gathered multitude and cheers and jeers, and certainly a surreptitious prayer or two. Perhaps, sometimes, ghostly echoes still drift into the nearby convent parlours.

It was the eve of All Saints, 1651, and the scaffold stood stark against a glowering October sky as the henchmen of Henry Ireton pushed their hapless victim onto the rough, splintering boards. Seconds later, as the cry of the crowd rose to a new pitch, followed by an uncanny hush, Terence Albert O'Brien, Bishop of Emly, Dominican Prior and martyr, was dead. For three hours afterwards, Ireton's soldiers beat his hanging body with their muskets.

Today in the Limerick Dominican community's memorial chapel the saintly Bishop O'Brien is remembered in stained glass by Murphy and Devitt and in two cherished possessions of the Order, the statue of Our Lady of Limerick and the beautiful Sarsfield Chalice, both closely associated with him.

There is also a small silver pectoral cross that was preserved for generations in the O'Brien family and said to have been handed by him to his mother just before his execution. The cross is of Spanish origin, made in the middle of the seventeenth century and depicting Our Lady and a crescent moon.

Terence O'Brien, a member of the noted family of O'Briens from the Arra mountains, was born in the castle of Turlogh O'Brien near Cappamore. In 1621 he entered the

The Bishop O'Brien Memorial Chapel, Limerick

novitiate of the Dominicans at St Saviour's in Limerick city, when he took the religious name of Albert, after the saintly Albert the Great who was the teacher of St Thomas Aquinas.

There was the customary year of intensive study at St Saviour's for the earnest young man from the Arra hills, after which, having satisfied themselves that he was firm in his desire for the religious life, his superiors sent him to continue his studies at Toledo in Spain.

Among the fifty or so Irish students listed in Spain at the time three others besides O'Brien were destined to become martyrs. These were Brother Arthur Geoghan, who was executed at Tyburn; Brother Thaddeus Moriarty, last Prior of the old Dominican Priory of Holy Cross, who was hanged, together with the patriot poet Pierce Ferriter in Killarney in 1653, and Brother John Collins, who was slain in Limerick a year after Bishop O'Brien's murder.

His studies completed in Spain, Terence O'Brien returned to Ireland, where his piety and administrative ability soon saw him appointed Prior, for one period at Lorrha, near

Portumna, and for two terms at Limerick. It was during his second term at Limerick that he was presented with the chalice that survives, a cherished possession of the Order, today. It bears the inscription 'Pray for the souls of Patrick Sarsfield and Eleanor White who had this chalice made in 1640. It belongs to the Convent of St Saviour's, Limerick, of the Order of Preachers.'

The donor, Patrick Sarsfield, was a nephew of the notorious Sir Dominic Sarsfield, who had condemned to death Sir John Burke of Brittas in 1606 for having allowed Dominican priests from Limerick to celebrate Mass in his castle on Rosary Sunday. Patrick Sarsfield was later appointed Recorder of Limerick and in 1640 he and his wife, Eleanor White, presented the chalice to the Dominicans in reparation for the deeds of his uncle.

Terence Albert O'Brien became Provincial of the 600-strong Irish Dominicans in 1642. Six years later, on a spring day, he was consecrated Bishop of Emly, his native diocese, in Kilkenny city by the Papal Nuncio, John Baptist Rinuccini.

Over the couple of years that followed, Bishop O'Brien was outspoken in his support of his persecuted flock, constantly being put under pressure by the arrogance of Inchiquin, 'Murrough of the burnings'.

With the seeping of power away from the Confederate Catholics, and the subsequent departure to Rome of Rinuccini in 1649, it became increasingly difficult for him to keep control of his diocesan affairs. In the resistance to Cromwell, he placed himself uncompromisingly in the front rank and he was the motive power behind the stubborn resistance when Limerick was besieged by Henry Ireton, the English commander.

Eventually, after five months, Limerick surrendered on 27 October 1651 and the Governor, Hugh Duff O'Neill, relinquished the keys of the city to Ireton. A triumphant Ireton told the Commonwealth Parliament: 'It hath pleased God since the surrender to deliver into our hands two persons of principal authority and influence in the obstinate holding out of Limerick, the Bishop of Emly and Major

General Purcell, whom we presently hanged and have set up their heads on the gates.'

Bishop O'Brien's arrest had been unresisted. Ireton's troops found him tending the wounded and those stricken with fever in a pest house on the north side of Mungret Street.

The last terrible moments were recorded by Ireton's second-in-command, Ludlow:

'A courtmartial was assembled and the Bishop of Emly and Major General Purcell were asked if they had anything to say why they should not die according to the sentence passed upon them. The Bishop said that, having many sins to confess, he desired time to prepare himself for that purpose, which was granted. Major General Purcell begged for his life, which was denied. The Bishop died with more resolution.'

At the 'trial' in St Mary's Cathedral, Bishop O'Brien had suddenly raised his voice and said that he was a bishop and all they could condemn him for was the faithful discharge of a bishop's duty and for that he was prepared to die.

It emerged later that, during the siege, Ireton had tried to bribe Bishop O'Brien to call the surrender with the offer of a free pardon and 40,000 gold crowns. The Bishop replied that Ireton himself would soon appear before the tribunal of God.

Henry Ireton died, filled with remorse, within the walls of the city he had captured ... exactly three weeks later.

The Rock of Cashel

Cashel, County Tipperary

Cashel — Cashel of the kings — may fairly be described as an exclamation mark on the landscape of Ireland. It is stark, dramatic, a majestic silhouette against the southern skies.

Certainly the most theatrical of all Ireland's holy places, the Rock of Cashel rears its precipitous bulk 300 feet above the Tipperary plains, its steep sides dropping away from a flat summit that extends for about two acres.

This remarkable, dominant focal-point was a superb site for the cashel, or stone fort, which was built there in the fifth century for the King of Munster and gave the place its name. It was the site also for one of the best known legends of Irish Christianity. It was here that St Patrick was preaching when he used the trefoil shamrock as an illustration of the doctrine of the Divine Trinity. Aengus, the king, believed and decided to embrace the new faith and was baptised.

Other years brought other personalities to this lordly grandstand that commands the rolling Munster countryside. In 1101 it was presented to the Church by Murtough O'Brien and the bishop of the diocese was raised to the dignity of archbishop. In 1172, after he had landed at Waterford, Henry II travelled from Lismore to Cashel to receive homage from many Irish leaders, including Donal O'Brien, King of Thomond. Edward Bruce marched as far south as Cashel and held a parliament on the rock.

The gem of the buildings on the rock is Cormac's chapel, a unique structure with two towers that dates from about the time an Irishman who had become Abbot of Ratisbon in Bavaria, sent a mission to his native land. Among the missionaries were several craftsmen who were to influence

The Rock of Cashel, rising above the plain of Tipperary

Irish church architecture. The chapel thus has a number of continental features, although its high-pitched stone roof on the corbel principle is in the native manner. It was built by Cormac Mac Cárthaigh, King of Desmond, in 1127.

The south wall doorway of the chapel has a carved stone tympanum depicting a huge beast being attacked by a centaur. The chapel contains a stone sarcophagus regarded as the tomb of King Cormac, although its estimated age does not endorse this. When the coffin was first discovered it was opened and found to contain the magnificent Cormac Crozier which is now in the National Museum of Ireland in Dublin.

The cathedral is a cruciform building without aisles, surmounted by a central tower approached by winding stairs off the south transept, and terminated at one end in a residential castle. It contains the inscribed wall tomb of Archbishop Myler MacGrath, one of the best known personalities in history.

The cathedral suffered damage in 1495 when it was

burned by Gerald, Earl of Kildare. On that occasion, when he was asked by Henry VII why he had set fire to the building, Gerald replied that he had done so because he thought the archbishop was inside! The king was amused and when it was remarked to him that all Ireland could not rule Gerald, Henry replied: 'Then he shall rule all Ireland!'

The cathedral was unroofed and abandoned in 1748, it is said, because its archbishop of the day could not drive his coach-and-four up the steep rock to the great west door!

The castle at Cashel, a plain rectangular building of three storeys, has walls thick enough to contain passages. The fifteenth-century, two-storeyed Hall of the Vicars' Choral was used for the accommodation of laymen or minor canons appointed to assist in chanting the cathedral services. St Patrick's cross is a unique form of Irish cross, the sides of which bear figures in high relief: the west side depicts Christ crucified, the east side St Patrick. Incidentally, the great stone base upon which the cross stands is thought to be the coronation stone used by the Munster kings.

Other features that must command the attention of the visitor at Cashel include the round tower, the oldest structure on the rock and extremely well preserved, the thirteenth-century Dominican Friary, with its beautiful east window, Hore Abbey, a Cistercian daughter house of Mellifont in County Louth, the eighteenth-century Queen Anne Deanery, once the palace of the former archbishops, Quirke's Castle, named after a family of printers who occupied it in the nineteenth century, and the Croke memorial cross on the former Milk Market, commemorating Archbishop Croke.

The ornamental fountain which stands at the south-west end of the Main Street recalls the extension of the railway to the town of Cashel in 1904.

Glenstal Abbey

Murroe, County Limerick

The monks first came to Glenstal in 1927, just about the time when, on the nearby Shannon at Ardnacrusha, Irish and German engineers were putting the finishing touches to the 'Shannon Scheme', the ambitious electrification development that was destined to change the face of rural Ireland.

Once their new foundation was firmly established, the Benedictines channelled their activities into a field in which they already had a long and distinguished record of achievement, that of education. They opened their school at historic Glenstal and before long its reputation had made it one of the most sought-after educational establishments in the country.

Glenstal today has its own high standards and it follows strictly the Benedictine principles. Intending students submit to an examination and then go forward for interview, after which the monks and the parents meet. Usually there are about 200 boarders at Glenstal and a long waiting list of others wishing to avail themselves of its renowned educational facilities.

Like other monastic foundations of its kind, Glenstal does not curtail its hospitality to students but is open to all comers. The inscription 'Pax' over its main entrance welcomes all travellers who seek its tranquillity and shelter. Frequent arrivals are small groups from the cities who come to Glenstal for weekend prayer meetings or to spend a few days sampling the traditional way of monastic life practised by the Benedictines.

When the monks first came to Glenstal in 1927, the massive Norman-Revival castle already had behind it almost a century of history. It was designed by a Londoner named

Glenstal Abbey, County Limerick

William Bardwell for the wealthy Barrington family who, in 1820, had founded the hospital of that name in Limerick City.

Bardwell spread his cloth generously to Barrington's unlimited wealth and came up with an imposing residence that had its own round tower-house and was approached by a huge gatehouse like that at Rockingham or Ballysaggartmore, near Lismore, County Waterford. The entrance was flanked by figures of Edward I and Eleanor of Castille, the queen bearing a scroll with the inscription 'Céad Míle Fáilte', an unusual acknowledgement of native culture by the landed gentry of the time.

Building commenced in 1837 but Glenstal was not completed until forty-five years later and its builders withdrew only in 1882. In exactly the same number of years ahead, the Barringtons were to give way to the Benedictines.

The monks found Glenstal an imposing backcloth to their work. Set in beautiful surroundings, close to the lovely gorge in the hills known as Clare Glens, its extensive grounds blazed with colour when the rhododendrons bloomed.

Among the outstanding features of the mansion itself were its octagonal library in the base of its round tower and an elaborate stone Celtic-Romanesque doorway between two splendid reception rooms, carved by local masons from

Newport and copied from a doorway in Killaloe Cathedral.

The monks of Glenstal have planted their own hallmark on this ancient estate that, even before the Barringtons came to build their fine new castellated mansion, had already carved its own niche in folklore.

In earlier days, when it was known as Cappercullen, the estate was owned by the O'Grady family and one reminder of them survives. On the west side of the approach avenue was the tree known locally as the 'Ilchester oak'. This was closely associated with a love story involving a beautiful O'Grady daughter and Lord Stavordale, a son of the Earl of Ilchester. The story goes that the young couple met at a ball in Limerick and fell in love. However, the romance met with parental disapproval on both sides. Love eventually triumphed, parents changed their attitudes and the boy and girl lived happily together ever afterwards.

St Finbarr's Hollow

Gougane Barra, County Cork

There is an old tradition of the Pass of Keimaneigh, the Deer's Pass, that tells us that it derives its name from the local legend that a lovely deer, a gentle creature, when hotly pursued by determined and bloodthirsty hunters, was endowed with an extraordinary strength that enabled the terrified animal to leap from one side of the pass to the other.

Not far distant is 'lone Gougane Barra', St Finbarr's Hollow, an island on a lake, joined to the mainland by an artificial causeway. Here, from this source of jagged mountains and towering cliffs, the river Lee trickles off to tinkle its way through enchanted Inchigeelagh and then gather strength to flow on through Macroom to distant Cork.

The pilgrim will find this holy place of Ireland about thirteen miles by road north of the head of Bantry Bay, where the lake snuggles into the ferns and crags just a mile from the main road that runs between Macroom and Bantry.

Here, in the seventh century, St Finbarr, patron saint of Cork, founded a hermitage on the tiny island. Although nothing survives of the original structure, there are extensive remains of monastic buildings of a later date, including a square courtyard flanked by ancient monastic cells.

There is a modern Romanesque oratory with stained-glass windows on which the traditional saints of County Cork are depicted. Close by, the courtyard, with its thick walls of rough masonry, is broken by eight recesses, each of which is furnished with a plain altar. There is an unique set of the Stations of the Cross with a text in Irish.

It is to Gougane Barra, to tread Finbarr's sacred stones, to follow the stations, to take water from the holy well, that pilgrims wend their way the year round, but especially

The oratory on St Finbarr's island, Gougane Barra

strong in numbers each year on St Finbarr's feast day, 25 September.

In the wide valley of the legend-rich Ouvane river, a wild place of precipitous crags and vegetation-blanketed slopes, and close to Gougane Barra, is the gorge-like Pass of Keimaneigh. Here, in 1822, a fierce battle took place in which the Whiteboys of Iveleary, an illegal tenant organisation, clashed with soldiers in one of the numerous skirmishes of Ireland's lengthy land wars.

Close at hand is Kealkil bridge with the dishevelled ruins of historic Carriganass Castle, stronghold of the doughty O'Sullivan clan.

This is a lonely valley guarded on each side by steep precipices quilted by wild flowers and with ferns thrusting out from every crevice. In the 1820s it was the impregnable stronghold of a gang of highwaymen led by a swashbuckling Captain Rock. Small wonder that ghosts walk hand-in-hand with saints at legend-haunted Keimaneigh and Gougane Barra.

Holy Cross Abbey

Sanctuary of relic of the True Cross
Thurles, County Tipperary

Throughout Ireland there are few more impressive ancient monastic settlements than this Abbey of Holy Cross that stands on the banks of the Suir river four miles south of Thurles.

Holy Cross, its very name commemorating the sacred relic it once housed, and redolent today of the glorious years of Ireland's early Christian tradition, was founded originally in 1168 for the Benedictines, or Irish monks of the Columban rule, by Donal O'Brien, King of Munster. It was transferred to the Cistercians about 1182. Because of intense rebuilding over the first three centuries of its existence, few of the abbey's Romanesque features survive today.

Early in the twelfth century, about 1110, a precious particle of the True Cross was presented by Pope Pascal II to Murtagh O'Brien, King of Munster and grandson of Brian Boru. This was eventually taken to Holy Cross where it was magnificently enshrined.

The abbey, in the years that followed, became one of the most popular places of pilgrimage in Ireland because of the precious relic. It was a centre of considerable ecclesiastic importance, its abbots for many years enjoying the status of peers of Parliament.

To the present day, in the south transept of Holy Cross, connecting two side chapels, may be seen the narrow passage known as 'The Monks' Waking Place', which is thought to have been the shrine for the relic. It has an elaborately groined roof supported by a double row of twisted columns.

It is unlikely, in view of the traumatic events of the years of suppression, that the relic would have survived were it

Holy Cross Abbey, County Tipperary

not for the close association between Holy Cross and the Butler family, the Earls of Ormonde. The fragment of the True Cross was entrusted to their custodianship, where it remained until 1632. For almost two centuries after that it passed through various hands until, in 1809, it was deposited by the Bishop of Cork with the Ursuline Sisters, in whose convent at Blackrock, Cork, it was held until the mid 1970s. It was then divided: part remained at the Ursuline convent while part was returned to Holy Cross Abbey, to be joined in 1977 by a further relic obtained from St Peter's Basilica, Rome. The two are held in a shrine at the abbey and may be venerated by the public.

For the surviving glory that is Holy Cross we are indebted to the Butlers of Ormonde. The fourth Earl, known as 'The White Earl', rebuilt much of it. On good terms with the Plantagenet kings who were his contemporaries and, indeed, five times serving as their Lord Deputy, he was a kindly and influential patron of the monks on the banks of the Suir. The abbey came under his protection officially in 1416.

Like so many other monastic settlements throughout

Ireland Holy Cross was suppressed in 1536, but about seventy years later the abbey and lands were made over to the Earl of Ormonde and the Butler family subsequently protected the monks, who remained there until the seventeenth century. It has recently been restored, with some work still to be done on its cloisters.

The church at Holy Cross has several beautiful windows, especially its east and west windows and the window in the south transept. On the epistle side of the high altar will be found the reconstructed sedilia of beautifully carved black marble, one of the most perfect works of its kind in Ireland. Close by is what is traditionally known as the tomb of the Good Woman's Son and, in the chancel, those of the O'Fogarty and Purcell families.

On a wall outside the abbey there is an inscription, surmounted by the arms of the Butlers and the O'Briens, testifying to the rebuilding of a bridge over the Suir by Lord Dunboyne and his wife in 1626.

Close to Holy Cross, incidentally, is Longfield House, once the home of Charles Bianconi, the Italian who introduced public transport to Ireland and who died there in 1875.

Mount Melleray

Trappist abbey at Cappoquin, County Waterford

Founded by the Trappist (Cistercian) Order in 1833 four miles north of Cappoquin, County Waterford, the monastic buildings and retreat houses of Mount Melleray stretch over the lower slopes of the Knockmealdown mountains.

It is hard to believe that the 800 fertile acres that are Mount Melleray today were once a barren tract of mountainside wasteland before being converted by the monks into splendid support farms for the settlement, stretching around the buildings the monks also raised here, their church, monastery, seminary and guest houses. All their needs come from their farm and dairy and auxiliary departments.

Mount Melleray takes its name from the Cistercian Abbey of Melleray, near the town of Chateaubriand in Brittany, founded in 1145 from Poutrond, a filiation of St Bernard's Clairvaux.

It was as a direct result of the suppression of the Chateaubriand monastery, laid waste by a force of 600 soldiers, that the Irish foundation came into existence. A group of sixty-four monks, fleeing from their devastated house, embarked on the battleship 'Hebe' and landed at Cobh on 1 December, 1831. They set up their new home in a small house at Rathmore, County Kerry. Here, under totally inadequate conditions, they followed their strict everyday routine, rising at 2.00 a.m., reciting the Divine Office at the usual hours and filling in their arduous day with alternating prayer and hard manual work.

The Prior, Father Vincent Ryan, immediately set about seeking a more suitable base. Within months he received an offer of a stretch of rough mountain land from Sir Richard Keane of Cappoquin. When Father Ryan saw it for the first time on a harsh, windswept February day, it was not a promising site, even for the austerity of a monastery. An early description paints the grim aspect: 'It was mountain land in the strictest sense of the term, rough and uneven in surface, covered with a thick dark growth of heather, furze and rushes; there were patches, too, where the heavy rains or the mighty force of mountain stream had worked away the thin surface of the peat and left nothing but the naked rock. Not a tree was to be seen over the whole extent of the area, nor a ditch nor a fence nor even a building of any kind except for a dilapidated gamekeeper's lodge at the southern extremity of the estate. "Scrahan" or "the coarse land" it was called and rarely was a name better suited to the reality.'

In the spring of 1833 the formidable task of transformation got under way, the monks reclaiming the mountain land and making it capable of cultivation. In the first year 17,000 young trees were planted, a visionary step that was to place the Mount Melleray of today against a dramatically different backcloth.

On 20 August of that year, the feast of St Bernard, the foundation stone of the projected monastery was laid by the owner of the land, Sir Richard Keane, at a ceremony said to have been attended by 20,000 people.

Less than two years later, on 17 May 1835, came the abbatical benediction of Dom Vincent Ryan, who thus became the first abbot in Ireland since the repeal of the Penal Laws.

A memorable day came for the monks of Melleray on 20 August 1838, when they welcomed to their new home on the bleak mountain slopes a most distinguished guest, no less a personage than the winner of Catholic Emancipation, 'The Liberator' himself, Daniel O'Connell. A description of that visit comes to us from an historian of the Order, Stephen Moloney, O Cist:

'As soon as the carriage bearing the Liberator and his secretary, Mr O'Neill Daunt, was seen approaching the Abbey gates, the bell rang out its peals of welcome and the entire community issued forth from the monastery in Processional order to meet the guests. Evidently the rite prescribed in the Cistercian Ritual for the reception of persons of eminence was followed. Leading Mr O'Connell to the Chapter-room, as the unfinished church was still in

The abbey at Mount Melleray, County Waterford

the hands of the tradesmen, the Abbot intoned the "Te Deum" which was taken up by the brethren and sung with great feelings of joy and fervour. At the end of the ritual prayers, an address of welcome on behalf of the community was read to the Liberator by one of the priests.

'On rising to reply, O'Connell was overcome with emotion; regaining his self-control in a few moments, he held up his hands and said: "My friends, these hands are stained with blood!" alluding obviously to the unhappy ending of his duel with D'Esterre. Then, thanking the brethren for their kindly reception of one so undeserving, and humbly begging a remembrance in their prayers during the days of retreat he proposed to spend amongst them, he retired to the quarters reserved for his use and spent a full week in recollection and prayer.

'Again on the morning that he left to return to Dublin, the Liberator delivered a touching address to the whole community assembled to listen to the charm of his words. Expressing his gratitude for the kind attention shown him during his stay, he praised the brethren highly for the wonderful progress they had made during the four years they had lived on the mountainside.

'Going back then into the history of the Irish Church during the recent centuries, he referred to it as a mighty victory of Ireland's faith over the Evil One. Exhorting the monks to revive among themselves the spirit of ancient Irish monasticism and recommending himself and his country's interests to their prayers, he promised to repeat his visit annually.

'This promise he did not fulfil. Distance from the capital, as well as innumerable engagements in the service of his country and of others, prevented O'Connell ever from returning. But the memory of him has never left the place and will be proudly retained as long as Cistercians dwell in Mount Melleray.'

Mount Saint Joseph's

Cistercian abbey, Roscrea, County Tipperary

The fine mansion of Mount Heaton, now the guesthouse of Mount St Joseph's, was built for a Cromwellian officer named Edward Heaton; it was once lost, they say, to the Prince Regent during a game of cards. A later owner of the splendid castellated house called Mount Heaton, Mr W.H. Armstrong, put it on the market in 1817.

After almost another sixty years in private ownership, it came up for sale again in 1875. This time it was bought by Count Arthur Moore, MP, of Mooresfort, Lattin, County Tipperary. He acquired it in order to establish another Trappist monastery in Ireland besides Mount Melleray. Having obtained the consent of Abbot Fitzpatrick of Mount Melleray, Moore realised his laudable ambition by handing Mount Heaton over to the Trappists on 1 March 1878.

On an eventful day in that same year, a party of thirty-three monks, including eight priests, travelled from Mount Melleray to Mount Heaton and, to commemorate the month it came into their possession, changed its name to Mount St Joseph's. The first Superior of the new community was Very Rev. D. Athanasius Donovan, who had been Procurator at the mother house.

The tasks that confronted the monks during their early years at the former Heaton mansion were formidable. Over decades of neglect the house, outbuildings and grounds had deteriorated into a sorry state of disrepair. There was dampness and decay everywhere, with crumbling walls, worm-eaten woodwork and leaking roofs. Gradually, however, they swung into a plan of restoration and a welcome transformation took shape. They converted the basement area into kitchens, refectory and cowl halls, the ground-floor rooms into chapels and a Chapter room, while the top floor served as a dormitory.

The abbey and guesthouse (background) at Mount St Joseph's, Roscrea

On Monday, 24 March 1879, Lord Abbot Fitzpatrick of Mount Melleray arrived at his Order's new settlement to lay the foundation stone of the church there which was dedicated by Coadjutor Bishop Ryan of Killaloe on 18 September 1881. Three years later came another red-letter day for the Trappists of Roscrea, when their church was consecrated by Bishop O'Callaghan, OP, of Cork, assisted by Bishop Ryan, the Abbots of Mount Melleray, Melleray in France, Mount St Bernard in England and Gethsemani in the United States.

The church was worthy of the dedication and enthusiasm that was forming the new Trappist campus, with its stout limestone pillars, graceful Gothic arches, clerestory windows and choir, the impressive centre of the colony's devotion.

Under the strict Trappist rules that obtained at Mount St Joseph's, women were allowed access only to the outermost section of the church. Men, however, could pass beyond the 'crossing' over which was the rood-screen, surmounted by a crucifix, and they could then enter the larger portion, which contained the choir, stalls and the magnificent organ, usually played by one of the monks.

South of the church there were two quadrangles, around which were situated the library, Chapter room, sacristy, refectory, dormitory, scriptorium and the infirmary. The Chapter room was in daily use for all meetings of the monks, presided over by the abbot and where all regulations were promulgated. It is acknowledged as being one of the finest Chapter rooms of any abbey anywhere in the world.

Mount St Joseph's, in the firm traditions of Mount Melleray, soon became a vibrant self-sufficient community, with its own stables, forge, dairy, bakery and laundry. In later years, a silk farm was started which was then the only one of its kind in Ireland. The boys' boarding school at Mount St Joseph's was to become one of the most prestigious educational establishments in the country.

Bishop Ryan of Killaloe, who played such an active part in the foundation of the new monastery, was anxious that it should be raised to the dignity of an abbey and he made frequent requests to the Pope that this should be done. Pope Leo XIII acceded to his plea by a Brief issued in 1884. In October 1887 Right Rev. J. Camillus Beardwood, a professed priest of Mount Melleray, was solemnly consecrated abbot.

Count Arthur Moore, when he decided that Roscrea should be the setting for the new Trappist monastery he hoped for, had picked a site of long-established religious importance. As far back as the seventh century, St Cronan had founded a monastery in a picturesque setting between the Devil's Bit hills and the Slieve Bloom mountains. There, too, were the ruins of a fifteenth-century Franciscan friary and, a couple of miles away to the east, the remains of the Romanesque Mona Incha Abbey, its beginnings clouded in uncertainty, its credits hovering between St Cronan, St Canice and St Ciaran.

The religious importance and antiquity of Roscrea is recalled in the Book of Dimma, which belonged to the ancient Roscrea Abbey. It contains a copy of the gospels and a Missa Infirmorum and is enclosed in a brass shrine mounted with silver plates and ornamented with Celtic tracery. It may be seen in Trinity College, Dublin.

Skellig Michael

Ancient Christian island foundation off the Kerry coast

Of all the lonely islands off the west coast of Ireland that attracted the anchorite monks of the early Celtic Church, none proved more satisfying in its terrible isolation than the lonely rock eight miles off the coast of County Kerry known as Skellig Michael. Because of its ancient monastic remains, for centuries the island has been called 'the most western of Christ's fortresses'.

Skellig Michael, sometimes called the Great Skellig, is a mass of precipitous rock, half a mile long by a quarter of a mile wide, and is one of two islands known as the Skelligs. The Little Skellig is seldom visited, as access is extremely difficult. Even in favourable conditions, landing on Skellig Michael is hazardous.

The remoteness of the little island holds a haunting attraction. It was called Skellig Michael after the Archangel Michael, patron saint of high places, appropriately, because it has a peak altitude of 705 feet in the south-west and 610 feet in the north-east. Its monastic buildings are perched on a rocky ledge about 550 feet above sea level.

The brooding isolation emphasises the extraordinary ascetic standards of the island's early monastic lifestyle. Yet this isolation did not always protect its saintly inhabitants. It did not save Skellig Michael from the marauding Vikings who made at least four onslaughts on it in the early years of the ninth century. The forays are recorded in the ancient Annals of Ulster, where we are told that during one of these skirmishes the storming Vikings abducted the Abbot of Skellig and allowed him to die of starvation while in captivity.

For many centuries the lonely island attracted multitudes of pilgrims from all over Europe. The austere penances they

Stone cross and beehive cells on Skellig Michael

performed there called for the pilgrim to have a good head for dizzy heights and the courage and physical ability to climb up to the narrow platform high on the sheer side of the peak. The pilgrim's culminating act of devotion was the recitation of the Pater Noster. It was then customary to kiss the cross, roughly carved in stone, that projects at right angles from the highest pinnacle of the rock.

Today visitors to Skellig Michael may leave the mainland at any one of several departure points: Caherciveen, Derrynane (birthplace of Daniel O'Connell), Portmagee or Knightstown on Valentia Island. It was from Valentia, incidentally, that the first Atlantic cable, linking America with Europe, was laid in 1866. From a boat making its hazardous way out to the island there are superb views of the majestic cliffs of the Iveragh peninsula, which in places rise steeply to almost 900 feet.

The voyage out to Skellig Michael is an awe-inspiring experience in itself. The rocky outcrops that skirt the little island have been carved by sea and weather into fantastic shapes, rough, jagged, inhospitable. The only landing place is a little cove close to the north-east peak.

The ruins of the abbey on Skellig Michael stand at 540 feet, on a small green plateau known as 'Christ's Saddle'. A sharply rising pathway, built more than 1,000 years ago and with more than 600 steps, leads to a flat area in the north-east of the island. This measures about 100 by 35 yards and has a protecting wall on the cliff-edge. Here there are five beehive cells, rectangular internally and clustered together, with roofs formed of overlapping stones.

Above the cells a tiny oratory perches defiantly on the high cliff edge. This is similar in construction to the cells, with a tiny window opposite the door. From this plateau, on a day free of mist, the view of the Kerry coast is breathtaking.

On a lower level, the pilgrim finds a lonely sixth beehive cell, a second oratory, some cemeteries with rude crosses, two holy wells and the church of St Michael, a building of later date than the rest.

Skellig Michael is, like Little Skellig, an important bird sanctuary, agitated always by the coming and going of puffin, fulmar, razorbill, kittiwake, guillemot, Manx shearwater and stormy petrel.

The monastic ruins on Skellig Michael are the most perfectly preserved remains of an early Christian settlement to be found anywhere in Western Europe. One can well understand the monks of old who sought out the silences of the Skelligs. Could one be closer to God's heart than on these Atlantic-washed knobs of rock off Ireland's lonely west coast?

St Mary's Cathedral, Killarney

Pugin's magnificent legacy

St Mary's, Killarney, County Kerry, must be one of the most beautiful and imposing cathedrals in Ireland. Designed by Pugin, it is considered to be the best and most important of his Irish churches and, according to the evidence of his own son, the one that was nearest to his heart. The talented architect (1812-52), who supplied the detailed drawings for the British Houses of Parliament in London, designed more than sixty churches.

When the committee formed to undertake the provision of a new cathedral for the diocese of Kerry — the old one lay in ruins at Ardfert — called in the services of Augustus Welby Northmore Pugin to undertake the task, they had merely £900 in hand. Even in 1840 that was no princely sum when the target was a new cathedral.

However, ready help came from the local 'Great House' when its lord and master, Lord Kenmare, who happened to be a Catholic, gave the committee £2,000 and left a further £500 for the project in his will. By 1846, the sum of £6,000 had been collected. Within two years Pugin had completed the first drawings and the site for the new cathedral had been marked off and cleared, just outside the town.

It was a full fifteen years after Pugin had first been approached that St Mary's was consecrated. The ceremony took place on Friday, 24 August 1855. By then a sum of £20,000 had been collected and the results were imposing. They so impressed a local journalist attending the consecration ceremonies that he wrote in the *Tralee Chronicle* that week that it was 'more like a dream of the middle ages than a thing of modern reality.'

There was one sad aspect of that consecration day. Augustus Pugin had died of strain and overwork three years earlier. However, the ceremony was attended by his son

Pugin's magnificent cathedral in Killarney

Edward who had continued his father's work, helped by a most distinguished architect, J.J. McCarthy.

Pugin had not been able to get to Killarney as often as he would have liked during the building of the cathedral. He was so much concerned with the project, nevertheless, having drawn his inspiration for it from the impressive ruins of the old cathedral at Ardfert, that he insisted on all work progressing only under the supervision of a Wexford man named Richard Pierce, in whose skill and ability he had great faith.

Further work was done on St Mary's over the early years of the twentieth century, including the building of the 285ft spire that towers over this spiritual centre of a sprawling and incredibly beautiful diocese.

Killarney being a premier Irish tourist attraction, Pugin's St Mary's has been seen and admired by many, from the historian Lord Macaulay, who said of that enchanted corner of County Kerry: 'I never in my life saw anything more beautiful', to the distinguished American writer and broadcaster, Archbishop Fulton Sheen, who greatly admired it when he visited the south of Ireland.

Archbishop Sheen was impressed by the cathedral and apparently enjoyed himself in Killarney. Like many a tourist before him, he came back with a story: 'I remember once being taken around Killarney by a charming driver. After the ride, I inquired how much I owed. They never tell you, nor give you a direct answer. He said: "You know how it is! I have a wife and ten children!" So I give him what was considered a fair rate and a really good tip. Whereupon he took off his coat, threw it over the horse's head, and said: "Father, I would be ashamed to let that horse see you giving me this." '

St Mary's Cathedral has been specially adapted to the liturgical dictates of Vatican II. Extensive alterations were carried out in 1972 by a special committee consisting of nine priests and five elected laypeople. The artistic director engaged for the work at the time, Mr Ray Carroll, has left this comment on record: 'In redesigning the necessary new positions of the liturgy's elements and the elements themselves, we loyally sought to follow Pugin's thought and feeling. Where the inevitable conflict arose between Pugin's medieval philosophy of liturgy and the now-for-the-next-300-years established modern one, we deferred to Pugin in matters of mood (namely, his sense of the sacred and his sense of mystery); took into account the internal, inbuilt commands of his building; and simultaneously followed, as faithfully as we knew how, the new guidelines set down by Rome.'

It is surely by fortunate chance that a cathedral as noteworthy and important as Pugin's lovely St Mary's should be provided with a natural backdrop as beautiful as the great, peerless sprawl of Killarney and its surroundings.

Tomb of Paul Cullen, Ireland's first cardinal

Clonliffe College, Dublin

Paul Cullen, from the little Kildare village of Ballitore, became Ireland's first cardinal in 1866. He was to play a prominent part in drafting the text of the dogma of Papal infallibility at the first Vatican Council.

In Dublin's Pro-Cathedral, hundreds pass Thomas Frill's statue of him each day and it is doubtful if many give him a thought. A few miles away, at Clonliffe College, his heavily studded coffin reposes half-forgotten in a white-tiled vault, a fact probably unknown to legions of Dubliners. Yet his forthright and uncompromising attitude and dedicated service to Ireland and the Church through troubled decades earned him recognition as, perhaps, the most important Irish churchman of the nineteenth century.

His importance in the shaping of the Church in Ireland for nearly half a century, when he worked unselfishly and certainly uncompromisingly in the corridors of active Catholic service, cannot be overstated.

Paul Cullen was born in 1803 into a wealthy farming family at Ballitore, the picturesque County Kildare village near Athy. Related to James Fintan Lalor, the crippled Tipperary man who voiced such passionate nationalist feelings in the pages of the *Nation* and later edited the *Irish Felon*, he grew up in an atmosphere of intense patriotism. His father took part in the insurrection of 1798 and a number of his uncles and cousins were executed for their involvement in the same event.

He attended the flourishing Quaker school that had been founded by Abraham Shackleton in his native village. Later,

Tomb of Cardinal Paul Cullen, Clonliffe College

at fourteen, he was sent as a boarder to Carlow College where, forty years later, another young aspirant to the priesthood, and a namesake, James Cullen, from New Ross, was to follow in his footsteps and to go on to become a Jesuit and founder of the Pioneer temperance movement.

The year 1820 found him in Rome, studying at the College

of Propaganda. He was prevented from attending the seminary at Maynooth, County Kildare, because of his father's rooted objection to his taking the oath of allegiance to the Crown, mandatory for all students at St Patrick's at that time.

Following years of brilliant study, Paul Cullen was ordained in 1829, at the age of twenty-six, in the year of Catholic Emancipation. Immediately after his ordination, he was appointed Professor of Sacred Scripture and Hebrew at the College of Propaganda and, three years later, Rector of the Irish College in Rome.

Most of the next three decades was spent by him in the Eternal City, during which time he was a well-known Vatican figure, friend of both Pope Gregory XVI and Pope Pius IX. In 1842 he was recommended as the new Archbishop of Malta, but the suggestion did not receive full support in Rome.

In the meantime his interest in Irish affairs never abated and during the worst years of famine he was actively engaged in relief work to assist his fellow countrymen. In 1849, when the Papal States were abolished, he became Rector of the College of Propaganda and, a few months later, following the death of Archbishop Crolly, Paul Cullen became Archbishop of Armagh.

Back in Ireland after an absence of so many years he was able at last to take a closer part in the affairs of his native country, whose interests had never drifted far from his thoughts. He convened the first Synod held in Ireland since the twelfth century. It met at Thurles, County Tipperary and, when its statutes were published, an irate Queen Victoria in London urged that he be prosecuted.

Cardinal Cullen lived at 59 Eccles Street, Dublin, in a fine old Georgian house that had been bequeathed to him by the parish priest of St Michan's. Before he became a cardinal, he had lived at Belvedere Place, off Dublin's North Circular Road.

In the years that followed his work was prodigious. He built countless churches, hospitals and schools, the Mater

Hospital and Clonliffe College especially being monuments to his achievements. He fought constantly against the proselytising that was rife at the time.

Cardinal Cullen died on Thursday, 24 October 1878, at the age of seventy-five. It is an interesting sidelight of history that a nephew of his, Father Patrick Moran, who for some years acted as his secretary, was destined, less than a decade after his uncle's death, to become Archbishop of Sydney and Australia's first cardinal.

The cathedrals of Dublin

St Mary's; Christ Church; St Patrick's

Dublin is a cathedral city thrice over. St Mary's Pro-Cathedral, despite its titularly lower status, has long filled a fully-fledged role for the Catholics of the capital. Christ Church Cathedral and St Patrick's Cathedral, although Protestant today, were both Catholic before the Reformation.

When it was being planned at the beginning of the nineteenth century, it was intended that the Pro-Cathedral should be erected in Sackville Street (now O'Connell Street) on the site subsequently occupied by the General Post Office. This plan was abandoned, as it was felt, in the years leading up to Catholic Emancipation, that such a prominent location might hurt Protestant susceptibilities.

Instead, Annesley House, the town mansion of Lord Annesley, facing Lord Tyrone's mansion (now the Department of Education) in Marlborough Street, was acquired. It was bought for £5,100 by a middleman named Val O'Connor in 1803, just about the time Robert Emmet was dying in Thomas Street. The employment of a middleman in the purchasing of properties was a Catholic ruse at the time, aimed at outwitting any Protestant who might oppose the transfer into Catholic hands.

Although Catholic-owned now, the mansion was retained intact for more than a decade, being rented out to the army authorities for the accommodation of troops. Then, in 1814, an amateur architect, John Sweetman of Raheny, was asked to design the new church. Sweetman, who had lived on the Continent, modelled the facade of the building, with its six-pillared Doric portico, on the Temple of Theseus in Athens, while he fashioned its interior on that of the Church of St Philip de Reule in Paris. It was to be his only work.

*Dublin's cathedrals — the interior of St Mary's Pro-Cathedral (above)
and St Patrick's (below) and Christ Church (overleaf)*

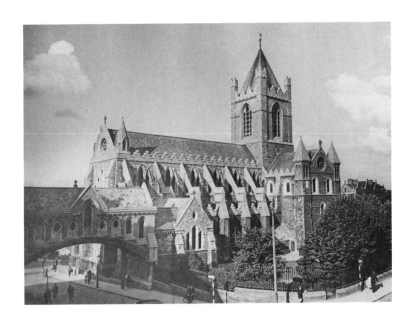

The first stone was laid on 28 March 1816. The imposing Greek Doric church took shape and was completed in 1825. It is thought that Sweetman may have been assisted by T.B. Keans and Sir Arthur Morrison.

When the new church opened its doors just before the dawn of Catholic Emancipation, it was first known as St Mary's Metropolitan Catholic Church and as such it began its continuing role serving the Catholic citizens of Dublin as their major place of worship. Many former Archbishops of Dublin rest in its crypt.

The Cathedral of the Holy Trinity, or Christ Church, was founded by Sitric, the Norse king of Dublin, about 1038 on the site of an early Celtic foundation on the south bank of the river Liffey. Today ruins in the grounds are those of the Chapter House of an Augustinian priory that was attached to the cathedral up to the time of the Reformation. The seat of a bishopric, it was not recognised at first by the Irish Church but was, in fact, subject to the Archbishop of Canterbury.

On the appointment of an Irishman, Laurence O'Toole,

as bishop in 1162, the diocese was linked to the Irish Church and Bishop O'Toole was promoted to the status of Archbishop of the province. He then converted the cathedral into a priory, the old community of secular clergy being supplanted by Aroasian Canons.

In the aftermath of the Anglo-Norman invasion, Richard Gilbert de Clare, better known as Strongbow, together with other Anglo-Norman leaders, built the present cathedral. Thereafter it ranked as the Priory and Cathedral Church of the Holy Trinity until the Reformation when, at the dissolution of the monasteries, a Dean and Chapter were substituted for the Prior and regular Canons.

Down all its years, Christ Church has seen stirring events played out within its walls. It was there, one day in 1394, that King Richard II sat in state and received the homage of the kings of the four provinces of Ireland, O'Neill of Ulster, McMurrough of Leinster, O'Brien of Munster and O'Connor of Connacht, each of whom he presented with a knighthood.

In 1486, Christ Church saw the coronation of a King of England. This was Lambert Simnel, pretender to the English crown in the reign of Henry VII, who was crowned king with great rejoicing and with the full endorsement of the Viceroy, the Archbishop and the citizens of Dublin. Unfortunately, Simnel, on his subsequent return to England, was swiftly disrobed of his delusions of grandeur and ended his days, certainly in a royal palace, but only as a scullery boy.

Other years brought other personalities to Holy Trinity. King James II assisted at Mass in the cathedral on his way to the Battle of the Boyne. The tabernacle and candlesticks used on that occasion survive today, treasures of the crypt. A short while later, another king came. This time it was William III, who offered his solemn thanksgiving for his victory at the Boyne, demonstrating his joy with the gift of a magnificent service of plate to the cathedral.

During the sixteenth and seventeenth centuries, the vaults beneath the cathedral fell into ill-repute, serving as boisterous wine cellars and taverns, frequented by the human dregs of the city.

In 1870, at the disestablishment of the Church of Ireland, the cathedral was confirmed as the Cathedral Church of the Diocese of Dublin and Glendalough. Around that time, too, it was magnificently restored by a prominent Dublin distiller, Mr Henry Roe.

Today, under the third arch on the south side of the nave, a massive tomb effigy is said to be that of Strongbow. If true, it is surely fitting that this redoubtable invader who built the cathedral in the first place should rest within its walls. Of all those who came here down the centuries it is his name that is synonymous with this Cathedral Church of the Holy Trinity.

Legend lingers long in the tumbled streets of the Dublin Liberties. Not far from Christ Church, it is claimed, St Patrick baptised people beside a holy well close to the old Poddle River. Today they will show you the site of the holy well and a stone marks the spot, fittingly enough in the very shadow of St Patrick's Cathedral, under which the same Poddle flows, its marshy surroundings cheating the cathedral of ever having a crypt.

St Patrick, they say, built the original Celtic church on the site and, indeed, an earlier St Patrick's was mentioned in 1179 in a Bull from Pope Alexander III to Archbishop Laurence O'Toole.

Just over a decade later, John Comyn, Anglo-Norman Archbishop of Dublin, raised St Patrick's to the status of a collegiate church. In 1191, the building of a new church in the early English Gothic style was started. It was raised to Cathedral status in 1213 and its first Dean, William FitzWyth, was appointed in 1220.

There were troubled days ahead for St Patrick's. In 1316 a severe storm blew down the spire and the building was set on fire by enraged citizens. In 1362, there was a serious fire that destroyed the north-west end of the nave and the tower, a conflagration in which the cathedral bells also were destroyed.

In 1713, the cathedral got a new Dean. He was one Jonathan Swift, Prebendary of Dunlavin in County Wicklow. Today, two ground slabs recall his memory and that of Stella, the woman with whom he will be forever linked. Above all others who entered its portals down the centuries it is the author of *Gulliver's Travels* and the indignant Drapier whose name is associated with St Patrick's.

It is a delightful Dublin irony that, while a generous distiller was responsible for the preservation of Christ Church, it is to an equally magnanimous brewer that Dublin owes the survival of St Patrick's. For many of its years the Guinness family maintained it with a generosity most notably evident in the full restoration by Lord Iveagh, head of the Guinness family, of the cathedral choir. This was done over the years 1901 to 1904, under the direction of the distinguished Sir Thomas Drew.

Church of the Most Holy Trinity

The former Chapel Royal at Dublin Castle

In Dublin city, 1814 was an eventful year. There was an unprecedented snowfall that paralysed the place for almost a month. The city weavers got their new headquarters in the Liberties. The 'Female Penitentiary' opened on the North Circular Road and O'Connell Street (then Sackville Street) got a post office for the first time.

At Dublin Castle, beside the massive Record Tower, the splendid new Viceregal Chapel, or Chapel Royal, was opened for divine service.

Today, the former Chapel Royal is the Church of the Most Holy Trinity, since it was adapted to Catholic worship in 1943. This small but beautiful church, where Viceroys once knelt in prayer, has since been used regularly for the celebration of Masses commemorating the insurrection of 1916 and the gaining of independence.

Although it had been intended originally to build such a church, surmounted by a cupola, at the head of Parliament Street, this site in the castle grounds, where a small church had once stood, was eventually selected instead. The leading architect of the day, Francis Johnston, was called in to design it. He had already redesigned the Viceregal Lodge, then the residence in Phoenix Park of the viceroy and today Áras an Uachtaráin, home of the President. His work also included the Under-Secretary's Lodge, which later served as the Papal Nunciature until the late 1970s.

Construction of the new church began in 1807 and gradually the lovely little building took shape. Exquisite plasterwork adorned its interior, executed by the distinguished George Stapleton, who also did the superb ceilings of Belvedere House, now Belvedere College, in Gardiner Place.

The church was built of black Dublin calp in Early Gothic

The Church of the Most Holy Trinity, Dublin Castle

Revival style and around its exterior were carved ninety heads in Tullamore limestone. These were executed by one of the leading sculptors of the time, Edward Smyth, assisted by his son John. Included in these were the heads of St Peter and Jonathan Swift.

The official opening, attended by the Viceroy and most Castle dignitaries, besides many socialites from the haughty city squares, took place on Christmas Day 1814, which happened to fall on a Sunday. With its elaborate oak carvings and exquisite plaster fan-vaulting and figure-sculpture, it was soon a new source of pride for the preening capital city.

The Chapel Royal became the headquarters of the Order of the Knights of St Patrick, whose banners adorned its walls. The insignia of the Knights, sometimes referred to as the Irish crown jewels, later disappeared inexplicably from the castle on the eve of a visit by King Edward VII in 1907 and were never recovered.

The magnificent little church that had been a centre of the panoply of empire for more than a century ceased to be the 'Chapel Royal' in 1943. In that troubled wartime year, it was adapted to Catholic service and became the Church of the Most Holy Trinity.

Today it survives, silent in its teeming memories, a place of quiet prayer in the heart of Dublin city.

Clonmacnois

Sixth-century monastic centre on the river Shannon

Of all the great monastic settlements of early Christian Ireland, Clonmacnois, Cluain Mhic Nóis, or the Meadow of the Son of Nos, is perhaps the most celebrated.

Situated on the Shannon, four miles north of Shannonbridge in County Offaly, its widespread reputation for learning grew rapidly in the years after St Ciaran founded his monastery there in AD 548. It enjoyed patronage from several kings, especially the last High King, Rory O'Connor, who was buried at Clonmacnois in 1198.

With most of the other great ecclesiastic centres of early Christian Ireland it was to undergo recurring plunderings down the centuries. Clonmacnois was constantly under attack from, in turn, ambitious local chieftains, Norsemen and Normans. In 1552, almost exactly 1,000 years after the foundation of the settlement, it was attacked by the English garrison based at Athlone. Soldiers rampaged through the sacred buildings and carried off everything they could lay hands on, bells, manuscripts, images, altar vessels, treasures. They even removed the glass from the windows.

In 1647 an effort was made to restore the cathedral at Clonmacnois but the troops of Oliver Cromwell were soon storming through the monastic city and repeating the desecrations of 1552.

Clonmacnois today is a sacred place of memories and ruins. There are the remains of eight ruined churches, two round towers, three sculptured high crosses and portions of two others, the ruins of a castle and several hundred monumental slabs.

The grave of Rory O'Connor, the last High King, who did so much to foster the early Clonmacnois, is in the north-east corner of the chancel of the cathedral, and that of his father, Turloch, King of Connacht, is in the south-east

Ruined churches at Clonmacnois, with the Cross of the Scriptures in the foreground

corner. The cathedral was built in 904 by Abbot Colman and King Flann Sinna.

The tenth-century Nuns' Church is one of the finest specimens of Irish-Romanesque architecture in existence. Its west doorway and chancel arch were donated in 1167 by the penitent Dervorgilla, who had run away from her husband, Tiernan O'Rourke of Breifne. While the doorway is one of outstanding beauty, it is surpassed by the wonderfully carved chancel arch.

Among this cluster of sacred buildings on the banks of the Shannon are Temple Ciaran, a cell that contains the saint's grave, Temple Doulin, a larger cell, Temple Hurpain, or MacLaffey's Church, Temple Conor, founded in 1010 by Cathal O'Connor, King of Connacht, Temple Rí, the King's Church, and Temple Finian, the twelfth-century oratory dedicated to St Finian.

The castle, erected in 1214 by order of John de Gray, Bishop of Norwich, was destroyed in Cromwellian raids.

O'Rourke's Tower, named after Fergal O'Rourke, who died in 964, had its entrance twelve feet above ground level. When under attack the monks, carrying the monastery's treasures with them, could gain the safety of the tower with the aid of a ladder which they would then haul up after them.

The Cross of the Scriptures, or King Flann's Cross, at the west door of the cathedral, was erected by Colman over the grave of King Flann Sinna who died in 914. This bears a wealth of illustrative and ornamental carving and has two inscriptions in Irish: 'Flann, son of Melaghlin' and 'A prayer for Colman who made this cross for King Flann'.

The earliest of the Clonmacnois crosses is the ninth-century North Cross, only the shaft of which remains. The monastic site contains the most extensive range of inscribed sepulchral slabs of the early Christian period in Ireland.

A treasure of the ancient settlement is the beautiful Crozier of Clonmacnois, one of the best preserved Irish croziers in existence, now held in the Royal Irish Academy in Dublin.

Still visible at Clonmacnois are sections of the old Pilgrims' Road, the only road to the monastery in its heyday, which extends from the cemetery towards Ballinahown. The annual pilgrimage takes place on the feast of St Ciaran, 9 September.

Shrine of St Brigid

Faughart, County Louth

Faughart, in the quiet countryside four miles north of the town of Dundalk, County Louth, of all the holy places of Ireland, must be one of the most venerated. Long a centre of pilgrimage, it is the reputed birthplace of St Brigid, ranked with St Patrick and St Columcille as one of Ireland's patron saints.

Accurate details of Brigid's life are scarce and most of what we read about her today has its foundation in legend. It is said that she was the daughter of a slave mother and a noble father. Sold into slavery herself, she was bought by a druid but she converted him to Christianity and was re-united with her father. Tradition tells us, too, that she spent part of her early life on the mountain slopes as a cattle herd, just as the boy Patrick did, before she entered the religious life.

Before long, Brigid's father resolved to find a husband for her and arranged to have her marry the King of Ulster. The prospective royal bridegroom, however, with commendable understanding and generosity, realised that the cloister rather than marriage was the path towards which Brigid inclined. He therefore promptly helped her to set up a nunnery in County Kildare.

The new establishment grew rapidly and by the dawn of the eighth century it was part monastery, part nunnery, accommodating both monks and nuns. When it was thus functioning as a double house, the church shared by the two communities was divided down the centre by a partition. There were two richly decorated shrines, one to Brigid, the other to Bishop Conlaed, one of the foundation's earliest abbots. Each shrine was surmounted by gold and silver crowns.

Shrine of St Brigid at Faughart (above) and St Brigid's Well (below)

Brigid's generosity to the poor was such that she frequently gave the clothes off her own back to those who flocked to her convent door seeking assistance.

Many legends about her shine through the mists of the years. One tells how she saved and protected a wild boar. The animal was being hunted and, utterly exhausted, was on the point of being caught. It managed, however, to reach the entrance to Brigid's convent. Brigid brought the boar indoors and then sent a message to the huntsmen outside, telling them that animals had the right of sanctuary within the convent walls. The hunt had no option but to disperse. Brigid helped the frightened and exhausted boar to full recovery and it remained at the convent with the other animals belonging to the community.

The present shrine at Faughart was built in 1933 and contains a relic of the saint. To the south-west of the ruined church flows St Brigid's stream, long a place of pilgrimage, where pieces of cloth were attached to the surrounding trees and bushes in the tradition of such holy places. A rock bears an impression said to have been made by Brigid's knees as she knelt in prayer. It was long a custom, too, for pilgrims to take water from the churchyard well and then to drink it from a human skull as a cure for toothache.

Also in the old churchyard at Faughart is a large stone on the slope of a hill covering the traditional 'King's Grave.' This is thought to have been the place where the headless body of Edward Bruce, who was slain in the battle of Faughart Hill in 1318, was buried.

St Brigid died, tradition says, at Kildare on 1 February, around 525, and although she was thought by some to have been buried there, the distinction of holding her remains was claimed by the Four Masters for Downpatrick:

'In Down three saints one grave do fill,
Patrick, Brigid and Columcille ...'

Fore of the wonders

Ancient Benedictine settlement, County Westmeath

Fore, truly, is a place of wonders including, traditionally, water that refuses to boil and a river that flows uphill. Such traditions have their roots in antiquity and the past lingers still in this lovely little village three miles east of the town of Castlepollard in County Westmeath.

If you follow the road to Fore you will travel in the footsteps of St Feichin who founded a church here in the seventh century. Taking its name from Fobhar Feichin, or St Feichin's Well, the hallowed ground nurtured a large group of interesting antiquities.

St Feichin was born in the village of Bile in County Sligo in 580 and it was said that his renowned sanctity 'was foreshadowed at his birth by a miraculous light, which shone round the house where he was born and lighted up the whole neighbourhood.'

In the old graveyard at Fore the main focal point is the partly restored church, a splendid example of early ecclesiastical architecture. The west doorway is remarkable for its massive lintel, estimated to weigh over two tons.

'This magnificent doorway is constructed altogether of six stones, including the lintel, which is about six feet in length and two in height, the stones being all of the thickness of the wall, which is three feet,' Petrie said of it.

The western section of the church is a mausoleum, originally the cell of an anchorite named Patrick Beglan, but adapted in the nineteenth century by the Greville-Nugent family of Delvin. Here, remarkable cyclopean doorways are reminiscent of doorways found in Syria and are looked upon as links between the early Celtic church and the east.

Close to the church is another anchorite's cell (only the eastern section of the building can be truly called ancient)

Ruined church at Fore, County Westmeath, showing the west doorway

which consists of a tower of two storeys, the lower of which is vaulted. In the graveyard is an ancient cross discovered in 1912 and subsequently erected on its present site.

A quarter of a mile outside the village of Fore the majestic bulk of the Benedictine Abbey rears with its square towers and loophole windows. Founded for the Benedictines by Walter de Lacy in the early years of the thirteenth century, it knew many troubled days as well as years of peace. In the abbey grounds are the ruins of the circular columbarium or dove house (pigeon meat was needed as food for the monks in winter) as well as the remnants of a church.

Evidence of the remarkable antiquity of the settlement of Fore and its surroundings are to be found on every side. There are, for example, no fewer than nine ancient crosses to be seen within a one-mile radius of the village.

Close to the foot of the Ben of Fore (713 feet) there is a large motte, credited in local folklore to be part of early Anglo-Norman fortifications, while on every hand the visitor stumbles across the crumbling remains of walls and gateways which helped to fortify the medieval settlement of Fore and to protect its cherished Christian artefacts. On the west side of the Ben of Fore there is another ancient anchorite's cell, said to have been occupied as late as the eighteenth century.

Fore Abbey was besieged no fewer than eleven times between 745 and 1176. When Walter de Lacy rebuilt it in 1209 it was adopted by the Benedictine monks of the Monastery of Evreux in Normandy. Henry VI introduced an Act of Parliament that made the monks of Fore independent of France and subject only to their own prior. Towards the close of 1539 Christopher Nugent, the 'Black Baron of Delvin', laid waste the church and monastery and set fire to the buildings.

Glendalough

Monastic centre of St Kevin, County Wicklow

It is a fortunate combination for the visitor that one of Ireland's most important ancient monastic centres is situated in one of the country's loveliest beauty spots, beside two lakes in the heart of the sprawling Wicklow hills.

A young man of princely descent named Kevin came here early in the sixth century, it is said, to escape the wiles of the opposite sex and to seek closer communion with God on the shores of these lonely twin lakes beneath the towering heights of Camaderry and Lugduff.

At first Kevin lived in a tree on the north side of the Upper Lake, but later moved to an even less accessible home, a narrow cave set in the cliff face on the south side of the lake, accessible only by boat.

It was not long before his reputation for holiness and learning attracted followers from far afield and, to accommodate these, a church was built on the south side of the Upper Lake. The number of pilgrims continued to increase so Kevin moved to the lower end of the glen, where he set up a monastic city that was to flourish for six centuries.

Not surprisingly, as the fame of Glendalough spread, the settlement attracted other visitors besides pilgrims and hermits. Plundering Norsemen came and the holy glen was laid waste repeatedly. In the twelfth century came the man who, with St Kevin himself, is most closely associated with Glendalough, St Laurence O'Toole, who was Abbot before going on to higher office as Archbishop of Dublin.

Today Glendalough is a city of enchanted stones. Its oldest remains are those of the first building erected here by St Kevin, Trinity Church. The newest, St Saviour's Monastery, was founded by St Laurence O'Toole. This is noteworthy

The round tower and St Kevin's Church at Glendalough

for its Romanesque chancel arch decorated with dog-tooth, chevron, floral ornamentation and futuristic sculptures of human heads and animals on the capitals and bases.

The largest and most important building at Glendalough is the cathedral built in the seventh century and in use until the thirteenth century when the See of Glendalough was united with that of Dublin, a union that exists to the present day. St Kevin's Cross, a granite monolith 11ft high, stands on the south side of the cathedral.

Of special interest, too, are the three slabs set against the north wall of the chancel. One of these bears an interlaced cross with Greek crosses in circles in the two upper spaces. In two lower spaces are inscriptions in Irish: 'Or do Diarmait' (Pray for Diarmait) and 'Or do MacCois' (Pray for MacCois). Another slab here has a beautiful design of scroll foliage branching from its stem.

Perhaps the best remembered feature of Glendalough is the five-storey round tower, 103ft high and 52ft in circumference. The conical roof was long ago blown down, but this was rebuilt in 1876 with its original stones. St Kevin's House, more often referred to as St Kevin's Kitchen, is a double vaulted oratory with a later belfry.

Other notable points of interest at this holy settlement include the tenth-century St Mary's Church, with its massive doorway and lintel; the Priest's House, the mortuary chapel for the surrounding cemetery situated south of the cathedral, worth viewing for the tympanum over the doorway with a carving depicting three figures, one carrying a crozier, another a bell; and the remains of St Ciaran's Church, destroyed by fire in 1163.

Glendalough has always been a place where legend flourishes. The best known tradition connected with it concerns St Kevin himself. It tells us that the holy man's flight to his 'bed' in the cliff face in order to escape the wiles and attentions of pursuing females was followed by the arrival there of a determined young woman named Kathleen, with 'eyes of most unholy blue', who succeeded in tracking him to his hideout. Enraged by her enthusiastic overtures, the saint hurled her from the cliff into the lake.

A more charming legend concerns a scooped-out piece of granite known as the Deer Stone on the south bank of the river. It is said that a white doe was milked every day into the cup-like hollow to provide milk for a child Kevin had found in the Glen, where it had been abandoned by its mother.

The Irish Lourdes

Church of Mary Immaculate, Inchicore, Dublin

This grotto was solemnly opened on Sunday, 11 May 1930, in the grounds of the Oblate church at Inchicore, with High Mass presided over by the Archbishop of Dublin, Most Rev. Dr Byrne. It was a dull, rainy day, but the weather did nothing to diminish the enthusiasm of the crowds that flocked to Inchicore, a westerly suburb of Dublin, to march behind what was claimed to be the largest candle ever lit in Ireland.

Thus the Irish Lourdes came into existence. It was a massive replica of the grotto at Lourdes, where Our Lady had appeared to a young girl named Bernadette Soubirous in the early months of 1858. Built of reinforced concrete, 43ft deep, 130ft wide and 24ft high, and with a 'cave' interior 55ft wide, it rose imposingly in the grounds of the Oblate Church of Mary Immaculate. A statue of Mary Immaculate, executed in white Carrara marble, stood in its own niche close to a marble altar behind wrought-iron railings.

The cost of the new grotto was £6,000, a not inconsiderable sum in that drab year at the start of the depressed 1930s when Dublin city, although modest in its population of 410,000, was just about to gobble up the adjoining urban districts of Rathmines, Rathgar and Pembroke.

Crowds packed the church grounds, themselves capable of accommodating 100,000 people, and overflowed into the surrounding streets of Inchicore, gaily decorated for the occasion.

The preacher at those ceremonies marking the opening of the Irish Lourdes was Bishop McNeely of Raphoe, who took as his text: 'My dove in the clefts of the rock, and the hollow places of the hill show me thy face, let thy voice sing in my mind — thy voice is sweet and thy face is comely.' (Sn 2:14).

When they assembled that day around the grotto, Bishop McNeely said, they would witness a spectacle not unlike the moving scene which took place at the Lourdes grotto itself, and they would recall the story of the wonderful apparitions — a story that a sceptical and materialistic world learned from the lips of the child Bernadette.

But the link between Inchicore and Lourdes dated from almost half a century before that when an earlier grotto had been built in the Dublin suburb. This, known as the Little Grotto, had been constructed by a noted Oblate of the day, Father W. Ring. Travelling with the first Irish pilgrimage to Lourdes, which he led, in 1883, it occurred to him that an Irish Lourdes would be welcomed especially by those unable to make the journey to France. Consequently, upon his return, assisted by a Brother Malone, he built his Little Grotto. Thus began the long tradition of devotion and torchlight processions that were to grow in strength and fervour as the years passed.

Years later, in 1924, another Oblate priest, Father Michael Sweeney, on a pilgrimage to Lourdes led by Bishop McHugh of Derry and attended by most members of the Irish Hierarchy, conceived the idea of erecting a more imposing and worthy shrine at Inchicore. Four years later construction was started, undertaken with care and with meticulous attention to detail.

A member of the Inchicore community, Brother Patrick McIntyre, was sent by his provincial to Lourdes to study the formation and contours of the grotto at Massabielle. On his return home, work on the new grotto was started, most of it being carried out on a voluntary basis by local workmen.

In August 1928 the provincial of the Oblates, Very Rev. Joseph Scannell, assisted by Father Sweeney, now Superior at Inchicore, blessed the foundations. After two years of work, much of it carried out on a round-the-clock basis, the Irish Lourdes was completed.

At the subsequent opening ceremonies, Bishop Collier of

The grotto of the Irish Lourdes at Inchicore, Dublin

Ossory urged devotion to the Mother of God, which was never more necessary, he said, than in the world of that day. An Irish Lourdes would help to inspire devotion to Our Blessed Lady. It would create a centre in Ireland, for everybody could not go to Lourdes, he said.

The distinguished author and journalist Aodh de Blacam visited Inchicore shortly before the official opening: 'How shall I find the words? How shall I find words wherewith to describe my impressions of the Inchicore shrine?... There before us, like a great lead-coloured cloud in the sky, we saw what seemed to be the very grotto of Lourdes itself. Yes, faith has planted a mountain here at Inchicore!'

Today, at the entrance to the grotto, in the courtyard, there is a large bronze reproduction of St Peter seated in his chair, a copy of the famous statue in St Peter's, Rome. It is a memorial of the first organised pilgrimage from Ireland to Rome in 1893 for the Jubilee of Pope Leo XIII. Originally, it was intended to surmount the figure of St Peter with a gold crown and, as a result of an appeal for gold for this purpose, countless precious and valuable ornaments, medals and pieces of jewellery flooded in. It was said that one well-known Tipperary hurler presented his gold All-Ireland medal a few weeks after he had won it at Croke Park. One diamond alone received from a generous donor was valued at £600.

Eventually, for security reasons, no gold crown was ever commissioned; instead, the gold so generously donated was used to make a beautiful chalice, designed by the celebrated Dublin goldsmiths, Smyths. This is highly valued by the community and is used only on important religious occasions.

The traditional ceremonies at the Irish Lourdes continue with unabated fervour, especially the annual novena for the Feast of Our Lady of Lourdes and the colourful torchlight procession each year on 11 February.

'The Irish Lourdes goes on — alive and prayerful,' writes Rev. M.F. Buckley, OMI. 'The daily "visits" continue their prayerful song. The "annual novena" continues to attract its thousands.... It is the story of a truly unusual spirit between priests and people in bringing to actuality a focus of prayer worthy of God's dealing with his people. It is the story of the growth and establishment of a hot-line to heavenly intervention in everyday, not panic situations.'

Jerpoint Abbey

Cistercian foundation, County Kilkenny

The ancient walls of Jerpoint Abbey rise out of the rich Nore valley, just twelve miles south of Kilkenny city and about a mile and a half south-east of the walled settlement of Thomastown founded in the early thirteenth century by Thomas FitzAnthony, the Seneschal of Leinster.

Established in 1158 by Donagh MacGillapatrick, King of Ossory, Jerpoint survives today as one of the most complete Cistercian remains to be found anywhere in Ireland and among the most dramatic reminders of Ireland's Christian past, always documented most effectively in stone.

The first abbot to be appointed to the new foundation was Felix O'Dullany, who became Bishop of Ossory. He died in 1202 and his tomb is one of several of interest in Jerpoint. It is in the chancel and on it he is depicted holding a crozier that is being gnawed by a serpent. Close by, and close to the sedilia also, is a fifteenth-century tomb to the memory of Peter Butler.

Jerpoint contains many fine monuments, most of them well preserved. They include tombs of the Butlers and the Walshes of the fifteenth and early sixteenth century. Some of these depict St Michael the Archangel, a popular subject of tomb sculpture of the middle ages, as St Michael was considered as the one entrusted by God with the responsibility of bearing souls to heaven. Most of this work at Jerpoint is thought to have been done by masons from a flourishing school nearby at Callan.

The oldest parts of Jerpoint Abbey are the Irish-Romanesque chancel and transepts. The east window is fourteenth-century, the central tower fifteenth-century. The fifteenth-century cloisters, partly restored in recent times by the Board of Works, the official department entrusted

Sculptured pillars at Jerpoint Abbey, County Kilkenny

with such tasks, contain some interesting sculptures.

Jerpoint, like most monastic settlements of its kind, has known unrest and peril. In 1387 its abbot was fined for violation of the Statute of Kilkenny which prohibited the admission of Irishmen to its community.

The twilight of Jerpoint Abbey's days of glory came when

it was suppressed in 1540 and its lands, about 6,500 acres, were given to the Ormondes. Until then it had been a centre of considerable wealth and influence.

Cromwell came in the spring of 1650 and stormed nearby Thomastown, where he and his troops stayed for three days.

Despite such times of trauma, Thomastown today retains at least one worthy treasure. This, the high altar that once graced Jerpoint Abbey, is to be found in the Catholic church there.

The Madonna of Malahide

Malahide Castle, Malahide, County Dublin

The intriguing story of the statue that vanished is part of the folklore of historic Malahide Castle, eight miles from the centre of Dublin city. Once the ancestral home of the Talbot family, the castle and its extensive grounds are now a cultural and leisure centre.

Today, incorporated in the fireplace of one of the finest apartments in the castle, visitors may see an ancient and lovely wood carving of Our Lady in the splendid Oak Room. Around the statue lingers the story dating from the seventeenth century of how it mysteriously vanished when danger threatened, and later, just as inexplicably, reappeared when the threat had passed.

The Talbots lived in the castle from the time of Henry II, except for one brief interval when they were banished from it, and to which period the legend of the vanishing statue belongs. The family were driven from Malahide after the Cromwellian onslaught of 1649 and in 1653 a lease of the castle and its lands was granted to one of the Commissioners, the Norfolk barrister Miles Corbet. He had sat in judgment on Charles I and had signed the King's death warrant.

Just before Corbet's arrival at Malahide, a beautiful carved image of the Virgin, one of the treasures of the castle, vanished without trace. When Corbet left, about seven years later — rather hastily, when it became apparent that the restoration of the monarchy was inevitable — the carving suddenly reappeared in its old place.

Corbet fled, sailing from Duncannon on the frigate 'Oxford' in 1660, and made his way to London where he took his seat in the House of Commons. Later, however, his election to the Convention Parliament was declared void

The Madonna of Malahide over the fireplace in Malahide Castle

and he fled again, this time to Holland where he was arrested. He was duly tried, found guilty and executed on 19 April 1662.

Although his tenure at Malahide was short-lived, Miles Corbet, during his time there, is said to have taken the roof off a fine old church close to the castle itself and used the building as an outhouse for cattle.

This little church was remarkable for a monument to Maud Plunkett, who had married Sir Richard Talbot. She became famous in song for being 'maid, wife and widow' in the one day, when her first husband, son of the Baron of Galtrim, on their wedding day, was summoned from the altar to lead his men and 'scatter a gathering of the Irish', in which pursuit he was slain.

Perhaps some agency other than supernatural was responsible for the disappearance of the castle's lovely wood carving, fortuitously just before the arrival of Corbet, who most certainly would have had it burned or otherwise destroyed, and for its eventual safe return just as soon as Corbet had departed.

The castle was eventually restored to the Talbot family and they returned to live at Malahide. As soon as they did, they had the carving of Our Lady enthroned in a place of honour in the Oak Room, where it may still be seen. Our Lady also figures in another old tradition about the Talbots and their ancestral home. It is said that she appears in the Oak Room whenever danger threatens a member of the Talbot family.

Yet another colourful legend of the castle was recorded by the late Dr George A. Little, one-time president of the Old Dublin Society and the author of that remarkable little book of Dublin topography published in the 1940s, *Malachy Horan Remembers*:

'Below the Castle the dungeons and vaults of King John divide the gloomy space. Here, it is said, a sleepless Puck holds watch and ward. But there is a little stairway "leading to the sky" which also lets into the Banquet Hall through a low-lintelled door. This is Puck's thoroughfare .... In days gone by, an old housekeeper, Miss Todd by name, would render guests breathless by sweeping them aside with an imperious gesture of her arm and with the portentous announcement "Make way, please! Puck is passing!" A moment's silence and immobility, in which she seemed to watch the progress of the sprite, and then Miss Todd permitted the sightseers to continue on their way.'

The end came for the Talbots of Malahide when, following the death of the Earl in the early 1970s, heavy death duties forced the sale of the castle and its contents. Happily the castle itself was bought by Dublin County Council, thus assuring safe tenure in her position in the Oak Room of Our Lady of Malahide.

For those who wish to see the historic carving for themselves, Malahide Castle is open to the public all year round at a small charge, with special rates for old age pensioners and students.

Mellifont Abbey

First Cistercian house in Ireland

Six miles west of the town of Drogheda, County Louth, a cluster of ruins on the banks of the Mattock River, a tributary of the Boyne, mark the place where the Cistercians set up their first Irish abbey. The Archbishop of Armagh, St Malachy O'Morgair, established it, appointing as its first abbot a priest trained by St Bernard in the Cistercian rule at Clairvaux.

The building of the abbey was started in 1142, on lands donated by Donough O'Carroll, King of Oriel. Six years later, St Malachy was to die in the arms of his close friend, the first abbot of the new foundation.

In 1157 an impressive gathering of Church and civic dignitaries convened at Mellifont for the consecration of the abbey church during a great Synod attended by Cardinal Paparo, the Papal Legate; Gelasius, the Irish Primate, seventeen bishops and many important lay personalities. Fifteen years later, Mellifont witnessed the flamboyant arrival of Henry II to receive the submissions of O'Neill and other northern chiefs.

Towards the end of the twelfth century, Mellifont played host to Dervorgilla, wife of O'Rourke of Breifne, when she spent her last years in penance close by. When she died in 1193 she was buried at the abbey.

A poem by Thomas Moore records the elopement of Dervorgilla with Dermot MacMurrough, the deadly enemy of her husband, Tiernan O'Rourke. It happened in 1152, while Tiernan was absent at Lough Derg. MacMurrough appeared at O'Rourke's fort at Dromahair, and abducted a not very reluctant Dervorgilla. She would appear to have confronted the situation with some equanimity because she took with her the finest animals on her husband's land and

All that is left of Mellifont Abbey, with the lavabo in the background

the best furniture in his house. However, she was back at Dromahair, reconciled with her husband, within a very short time.

She and Tiernan were present at the consecration ceremonies at Mellifont in 1157, when she presented the abbot with sixty ounces of gold, a magnificent gold chalice and nine altar cloths. Ten years later, incidentally, she was to build the beautiful Hiberno-Romanesque Nuns' Church at Clonmacnois. On the death of her husband in 1186, she retired to Mellifont and died there in 1193.

The elopement of Dervorgilla proved to have been a milestone in Irish history, as it led to the flight of Dermot MacMurrough from Ireland and his subsequent arrangement with Henry II for an Anglo-Norman invasion.

In 1539, Mellifont, like so many similar settlements all over Ireland, was suppressed. About twenty-seven years later, it came into the possession of Edward Moore, who was afterwards knighted and who turned the church into a fortified residence. His son, Sir Garret Moore, a friend of Hugh O'Neill, offered hospitality and protection to Red Hugh O'Donnell following his escape from Dublin Castle a few years later.

The house at Mellifont was captured by Sir Phelim O'Neill during the siege of Drogheda in 1641 but later the Moores, afterwards the Earls of Drogheda, returned and continued to live there until 1720.

Today the ruins at Mellifont include remnants of the Gate House, with its massive square tower, the large abbey church, the Chapter House (sometimes wrongly called St Bernard's Chapel), thought to have been one of the finest of its kind in Ireland, and the interesting lavabo, where the monks washed their hands before going into the refectory for meals.

In the abbey church, under the remains of the sedilia, excavations revealed a tomb containing bones and a gold ring The ring was sold to a workman and was never recovered. Speculation broods over this historic burial place, that it may be the tomb of Dervorgilla or, alternatively, that of one of the two Archbishops of Armagh, Thomas O'Connor and Luke Netterville, both of whom were buried at the abbey.

A New Mellifont, and known as that, was established by the Cistercians in 1939 at Oriel Temple, the residence of the Foster and Massereene families, at the nearby village of Collon, County Louth. The house here was built in the 1780s by John Foster, afterwards the first Lord Oriel and the last Speaker of the Irish House of Commons before the Union of Britain and Ireland.

Monasterboice

The High Cross of Muireadach, County Louth

The journey of the pilgrim to Monasterboice, that once-vibrant monastic centre six miles north-west of Drogheda, County Louth, is richly rewarded, if only because it is here that stands the most perfectly preserved of all Ireland's ancient monastic high crosses, the Cross of Muireadach.

It was at this secluded and picturesque spot, only three miles from that other great Christian settlement of Mellifont, that St Buith, a holy man who was born in the district, built the church that was to bear his name, St Buith's Abbey.

Buith left his native land as a young man and, having studied in Wales, conducted missionary work among the Picts before returning to Ireland and setting up his own centre of learning on land granted to him at Monasterboice by a local chieftain.

Founded towards the close of the fifth century, the holy settlement expanded as its fame spread, but today all that remain are two churches, a round tower, three sculptured crosses, a couple of early grave slabs and a sundial, all set in the centre of an old graveyard.

The splendid Muireadach's Cross rises out of this historic earth close to the entrance of the graveyard at Monasterboice, a dramatic testimony to the fervour and craftsmanship of the holy men of such settlements during the dawning years of Christianity in Ireland. It survives today, a magnificent monolith 17ft 8ins high, every surface inch of which is covered with sculptured panels executed with superb skill from first-class designs.

The central sculptures of the cross depict, on its west face, Christ crucified and, on its east face, the Last Judgment. The sculptor apparently was not without a sense of humour, as the Last Judgment panel shows Satan helping the

Round tower and Muireadach's Cross at Monasterboice, County Louth

damned souls into the flames of hell with an enthusiastic kick.

In all, Muireadach's cross contains twenty-two sculptured panels bearing scenes from the Scriptures, human and animal figures, symbolic carvings and a delightful variety of interlaced designs. The lowest panel on the west side of the shaft of the cross bears the inscription in Irish: 'Or do Muireadach las ndearnad in chros' ('Pray for Muireadach who made this cross').

The Muireadach referred to is almost certainly the Muireadach who was Abbot of Monasterboice from AD 890 to 922.

Two other crosses at Monasterboice are the West or Tall Cross and the North Cross. The former is 21ft 6ins in height and is lavishly ornamented on every available surface. The head, on a separate stone, as it seems less weathered, would appear to be a later addition probably substituted for the original, which was almost certainly damaged by Cromwell's troops. The cross also contains a number of figure-scenes like those on Muireadach's cross, although some of these are impossible to interpret.

The North Cross stands 16ft high and also bears evidence of Cromwellian damage. The head is supported by a modern stem replacing the original which, broken, rests on the ground nearby. The west side contains a simple representation of the crucifixion, while the east face is adorned with a beautiful circular pattern of spirals.

Of the two churches at Monasterboice, the South Church is the older and the larger, dating from the ninth century. It has a rectangular nave measuring 39ft by 22ft, but of the chancel only shapeless mounds of earth remain today. The North Church is also rectangular, with no surviving trace of a chancel. It stands close to the round tower.

In the years of its glory, before its conical cap and some of its topmost stones disappeared, this round tower at Monasterboice was almost certainly the tallest in the country. It has five storeys, all now fitted with modern floors and protected from the weather with a concrete roof. It is 100ft high and is 51ft in circumference at its base.

Among the interesting smaller artefacts to be seen at Monasterboice are a sundial fashioned from a granite block, a common feature of old monastic cities, and a monumental stone with an inscription in Irish that requests 'A prayer for Ruarchan'.

The enthusiastic seeker of Ireland's past who visits Monasterboice will find it most rewarding to travel just one mile further northwards. Here, a fine example of a Bronze Age tomb, known to archaeologists as a 'Gallery Grave', will be found at Paddock, near Tinure. It is known locally as the Cailleach Béara's House. (The 'Hag of Béara' is a colourful figure in Irish folklore.)

Mother Mary Aikenhead

Sisters of Charity hospice, Harold's Cross, Dublin

Mary Aikenhead was born in Cork city on 19 January 1787, the child of a mixed marriage and a convert to Catholicism. Her father was a prominent Cork physician with many influential friends. One of the most dramatic occurrences in the life of his little family must have been the exciting night when his home offered refuge to a fugitive Lord Edward Fitzgerald, the nobleman turned patriot then on the run from Crown forces.

Mary was sent to foster parents, John and Mary Rorke, at Eason's Hill outside Cork, as was the custom then, about the same time as a child named Daniel O'Connell was being fostered out to a herdsman and his wife on his father's estate at Derrynane. She was to spend six happy years of her life with the Rorkes.

It was not until her father was converted to Catholicism on his deathbed in 1801 that Mary Aikenhead herself became a Catholic. She soon showed all the zeal of the convert.

Her enthusiasm for her new religion soon made itself manifest. In response to a call for helpers from Archbishop Murray, who was later to become Archbishop of Dublin, in the formation of an Order he was planning, The Congregation of the Sisters of Charity, she immediately volunteered.

Nobody was more surprised than the smiling Cork girl herself when Archbishop Murray, perhaps with an inspired focus on the future, insisted that she become the foundress of the new Order and its first Reverend Mother.

On a sparkling May morning in 1812, accompanied by another young woman offering herself in the service of God, Alicia Walsh, she made the journey to a novitiate in York.

Mother Mary Aikenhead's room at the hospice of the Sisters of Charity, Harold's Cross, Dublin

Three years later they returned to Ireland, the first Irish Sisters of Charity.

The convent they set up was in Dublin's North William Street, where they provided a home for fourteen orphans and opened a school for the youngsters of the neighbourhood.

In February 1819 she founded a community in Stanhope Street, where girls were trained in domestic work, while Harold's Cross got the Hospice of the Dying where, nearly forty years later, she herself was to die. With characteristic and unrelenting determination, Mary Aikenhead had tackled her most ambitious plan, the setting up of a hospital for the sick poor. For almost twenty years she had been unable to do anything practical about this dream, except to pray and to formulate plans that she hoped one day she might be able to implement.

Then, in 1832, it seemed that her prayers were answered in the most dramatic manner when a novice brought with her into the convent the sizeable dowry of £3,000, a considerable amount of money in that distraught year when cholera was raging throughout Ireland. Mary Aikenhead must surely have sensed the hand of God in the coincidence that the £3,000 she had just received was the exact amount of money needed for the purchase of the Earl of Meath's splendid town house on St Stephen's Green, which had just been placed on the market. She promptly bought the premises and, in 1834, St Vincent's Hospital opened its doors for the first time.

Her dream became a reality and her brave new hospital on the Green began its invaluable service to the city of Dublin. By that time, unfortunately, Mary herself was a semi-invalid and she was to remain so until her death.

Mary's physical disabilities, however, in no way impaired her capacity for planning and putting plans into effect. In 1838 she sent her nuns to work in the convict settlements of New South Wales, the first nuns to land in Australia, where they were eventually responsible for revolutionising the prison system.

The work went on, tirelessly, with dogged scorn for the physical setbacks that seemed always to be threatening it. It was not long before the Order could claim about thirty convents in Ireland, a dozen or so in Britain and others in the United States, Rhodesia and Australia.

Mary Aikenhead died in her own hospice at Harold's Cross in July 1858, carried to her grave by workmen who were doing so at their own specific request, their simple tribute to her for all she had done for the poor of Dublin. The decree for the introduction of the cause of her beatification was signed by Pope Benedict XV in 1921.

Time eventually ran out for the gracious Georgian mansion on St Stephen's Green that she had purchased with her novice's dowry. It was vacated in the 1960s, after more than a century of service to Ireland's sick. A new St Vincent's was opened at Elm Park, Ballsbridge, in November 1970, with 455 beds, at that time the largest general teaching hospital in the country.

The dream of a remarkable Cork girl had come, surely, to impressive fruition.

Our Lady of Dublin

Carmelite church, Whitefriar Street, Dublin

With the everyday noises of a busy shopping thoroughfare cut off by the stout walls of the Carmelite church in Whitefriar Street (see chapter on St Valentine, p. 109), a time-blackened statue of the Blessed Virgin, carrying the Infant Jesus in her arms, and known as Our Lady of Dublin, is perhaps the best loved shrine in the capital city, especially cherished by Dubliners themselves.

This ancient wooden sculpture has weathered many troubled and uneasy years as each century added its own particular patina to its durable surface. The stories that cling around it, like wisps of vapour that refuse to be banished, have, more than anything else, made it the object of veneration it is today.

This lifesize figure in oak is thought to have been carved in the sixteenth century. Although blackened now, it was originally painted in an assortment of bright colours, while later in its career it was insensitively whitewashed.

The statue originally occupied a place of honour in St Mary's Cistercian Abbey on the north bank of the Liffey. Although only the Chapter House of this structure remains today, its original floor much lower than present ground level, the abbey in its time was a fashionable place of worship popular with court officials.

In its Council Chamber, in the troubled June of 1534, Silken Thomas threw down his sword, declaring himself as being henceforth the king's enemy instead of his deputy. Five years later, when the Reformation came, St Mary's surrendered. The statue was then placed face downward and, hollowed out, used as a trough for pigs in the yard of a nearby inn. This could well have been done, not to show disrespect to the Blessed Mother, but with the deliberate

The shrine of Our Lady of Dublin, Whitefriar Street

intention of protecting the statue until more tolerant days dawned.

Endorsement of this history of Our Lady of Dublin comes in the earliest mention of it, to be found in a brief account of 'the Catholic chapel' of Dublin compiled by a Protestant in 1749:

'In Mary's Lane is a parochial chapel whose jurisdiction extends from one side of Boot Lane to one side of Church Street. It is a large and irregular building. On the Epistle side of the altar stands a large image of the Blessed Virgin with Jesus in her arms, carved in wood; which statue at the dissolution belonged to St Mary's Abbey.'

One of the colourful traditions hovering around Our Lady of Dublin concerns the silver crown that originally adorned the head of the statue. This was 'borrowed' in 1487 for use at the coronation of Lambert Simnel as King Edward VI of England in Christ Church Cathedral, but it does not appear to have been particularly lucky for this baker's son with regal pretensions as, upon his return to England, he was promptly arrested.

According to the distinguished archaeologist Petrie, he saw the crown offered for sale in the window of a jeweller's shop and described it: 'It was a double arched crown such as appears on the coins of Henry VII and on his only: a circumstance which marks with exact precision the age of the statue which it had adorned.' It is said that the crown was subsequently melted down and sold for the value of the metal.

The statue, now whitewashed, had by 1824 found its way into the window of a secondhand shop in Capel Street, adjoining the site of St Mary's Abbey, where it was seen by chance by Father Spratt of Whitefriar Street, who immediately purchased it for a small sum of money.

Father Spratt, who had been responsible for many improvements and innovations in the area, and to whom the Pope had presented the remains of St Valentine, carried the statue back to the then new Whitefriar Street church, where he placed it on the Epistle side of the high altar.

It was not until 1914, however, that the statue received the attention its history had earned for it. The whitewash that had been daubed over it was cleaned off and the figures were carefully cleaned. The arm of the Child, which was damaged, was restored.

The statue was then formally erected in the north chapel of the church where, today, it is venerated by Dubliners as their own special shrine, Our Lady of Dublin.

Our Lady's Island

Pilgrim island near Rosslare, County Wexford

There is a castle on 'the windswept shore' of County Wexford that is said to lean at a greater angle than the tower at Pisa and, if antiquity promotes such wonders, this is hardly surprising for the site, as a stronghold of defence, goes back to the time of the Crusades.

The first castle erected on Our Lady's Island was built by the redoubtable Rudolph de Lamporte who, in 1184, threw in his lot with the second Crusade and set off for the Holy Land, only to be slain the following year at the battle of Hattin.

Today, Our Lady's Island is less renowned for geometrically unstable artefacts or gallant Crusaders than as a place of pilgrimage and the great annual demonstration of faith that takes place from 15 August, the Feast of the Assumption and the principal day of pilgrimage, to 8 September, Our Lady's birthday.

Our Lady's Island is not really an island, being joined to the mainland by a causeway. On an inlet of the sea called Our Lady's Island Lake, near Carnsore Point and five miles south of Rosslare, it has been for centuries the most celebrated place of pilgrimage in County Wexford.

The island was the site of an ancient monastery dedicated to the Blessed Virgin and it has the ruins of a thirteenth-century Augustinian Abbey of St Mary and the crumbling ruin of a Norman castle.

Down the centuries, the pilgrimage tradition of Our Lady's Island continued; the restrictions and hazards of the Penal Laws, rather than evaporating the ardour it inspired, promoted the demonstrations of faith there, just as they did in so many other holy places throughout Ireland. On one occasion, in those years of the persecution of Catholics, English soldiers stormed through the island and threw

An aerial view of Our Lady's Island, County Wexford

crucifixes, statues and any other sacred objects they could lay hands on into the lake.

The prescribed formula of pilgrimage on the island is for pilgrims to walk slowly around, reciting the Rosary and other prayers, and then to wade barefoot through the water on the shore.

For more than 500 years pilgrimages to Our Lady's Island were organised by the Canons of St Augustine, but in modern times they were taken over by the Diocese of Ferns. While devotion fell off during the nineteenth century, there was a marked revival about 1897 which continues today.

At nearby Carnsore Point are the remains of the church and holy well of St Vauk, or Veoc, an Irish saint who died in Brittany in AD 585 and who is still venerated there.

A short distance west of Our Lady's Island, at Ballysampson, Tacumshane, the 'father of the American navy', Commodore John Barry, was born. Today his statue stands on the quayside in Wexford town.

Shrine of St Oliver Plunkett

St Peter's Church, Drogheda, County Louth

Drogheda, thirty miles north of Dublin, is a historic town situated on the river Boyne where it marks the boundary between Counties Louth and Meath. As a settlement, it dates from earliest times, when its name was Inver-Colpa, the Port of Colpa. When the Norse established a permanent township there in 911, they started its growth in importance.

Henry IV granted the town a charter, Richard II set up court there, Phelim O'Neill stormed its walls in vain, Cromwell massacred its garrison, attacking the town from a mound behind the workhouse, and, after the battle of the Boyne, William marched triumphantly through its narrow streets.

Occasionally, Parliament met in Drogheda and it was there, in 1495, that Poyning's Laws were enacted, providing that in future the Irish Parliament should pass no law not approved by the English Privy Council. Drogheda Corporation was once granted the right to issue its own coinage and the town also received permission to constitute a university with the same privileges as Oxford University, but this was never availed of because of the poverty of the times and the lawless state of the country.

Today, however, the town of Drogheda, arguably a city by virtue of ancient rights, is perhaps less closely associated with the striding personalities of its turbulent past than with that man of peace, St Oliver Plunkett.

The epicentre of Drogheda's homage to St Oliver Plunkett is St Peter's Church in West Street. This proud-spired Gothic building was erected as a memorial to the martyr of Tyburn and, in a special shrine within, his head is preserved and venerated.

Oliver Plunkett was born into a noble family at

The shrine of St Oliver Plunkett, Drogheda, with (inset) the head of the saint

Loughcrew, near Oldcastle, County Meath, about thirty miles west of Drogheda, in 1625. He studied for the priesthood in Rome, at the Irish College that had been co-founded by Father Luke Wadding. He returned to Ireland on his appointment as Archbishop of Armagh.

Realising that the Church in Ireland was deteriorating rapidly, the new Primate set about restoring it by embarking upon a comprehensive plan of widespread Confirmations and Ordinations as well as educational schemes.

He clashed with Archbishop Talbot of Dublin, who challenged him for the Primacy, but they were reconciled just before Talbot's death.

In 1679, Plunkett was accused of being involved in the Popish plot to land a French army in Ireland. Although he was imprisoned in Dublin Castle, his subsequent trial had to be abandoned when vital witnesses failed to show up. The following year, the Archbishop was taken to London to stand trial there. During the following months, while a determined effort was being made by the authorities to marshal enough witnesses to convict him, he languished in Newgate Jail, that grim London fortress developed, surprisingly, by Dick Whittington!

Eventually, on the testimony of a batch of degenerate 'witnesses', Plunkett was convicted and sentenced to death. On the first day of July 1681 he was hanged, drawn and quartered at Tyburn.

For almost two centuries, the Archbishop's severed head remained in the care of the Dominican nuns in Drogheda. In 1921, it was placed in a shrine in St Peter's Church on West Street. Preserved there, too, is the door of Plunkett's cell at Newgate. Oliver Plunkett was canonised by Pope Paul VI in St Peter's Square in Rome on Sunday, 12 October 1975.

In the early autumn of 1979, Pope John Paul II spent three days in Ireland. One of the chief places he visited was Drogheda. It was there that he said:

'St Oliver Plunkett, Primate of Ireland for twelve years, is for ever an outstanding example of the love of Christ for all men. As bishop, he preached a message of pardon and peace. He was, indeed, the defender of the oppressed and the advocate of justice, but he would never condone violence. For men of violence his word was the word of the Apostle Peter: "Never pay back one wrong with another".

'As a martyr for the faith, he sealed by his death the same message of reconciliation that he had preached during his life. In his heart there was no rancour, for his strength was the love of Jesus, the love of the Good Shepherd who gives his life for his flock. His dying words were words of forgiveness for all his enemies.'

Shrine of St Valentine

Carmelite church, Whitefriar Street, Dublin

It was the year that Dublin city acquired such noteworthy institutions as the Dublin Choral Society, the Dublin Mechanics Institute and, on the northside's Portland Row, what was called, in the quaint terminology of the day, 'St Joseph's Asylum for Aged and Virtuous Single Females'.

On 10 November 1836, the Archbishop of Dublin, Dr Murray, drove across the city to the new Carmelite church in Whitefriar Street to preside at a High Mass marking the arrival there of the remains of the young Roman martyr Valentine.

It was a moving chapter in the chequered story of the Carmelite Fathers in Dublin and, in the history of their splendid new church in Whitefriar Street, an early episode in what today stands as more than a century and a half of stirring service to the city.

The church had been built on the site of a pre-Reformation priory, for the Carmelites already had a long Dublin history behind them. In medieval times they had houses in numerous places around Ireland, from Dublin to Ardee, from Thurles to Rathmullen.

In 1333, the old priory that stood on the same Whitefriar Street site was used as a meeting place for the Irish Parliament. By the beginning of the nineteenth century the Carmelites had established themselves in many areas of Dublin city. Among these were Ashe Street in 1728, Upper Mercer Street, then known as French Street, and Cuffe Lane in 1806.

Although there were at the time no more than twenty-six Carmelites in the whole of Ireland, eight of these working in Dublin, it was decided to build a new church. The

Shrine of St Valentine, Whitefriar Street, Dublin

foundation stone was laid in 1825 and the building was completed in 1827, two years before Catholic Emancipation, the architect being George Papworth. The entire cost was £4,000.

Nothing can be said of the early years of the church in Whitefriar Street and the years leading up to its construction without mention of the man who was the dominant figure among Dublin Carmelites of the period and who was later to be responsible for the close association with St Valentine.

The remarkable John Spratt was a Dubliner and, like so many young Irishmen at the time aiming at the priesthood, was educated on the Continent. He was received into the Carmelite Order at Cordova in Spain. Back in Dublin, Father Spratt opened a school in Longford Street in 1822 and, because of the demands upon it, was forced to transfer to larger premises at Whitefriar Street two years later. The community moved there in 1825 when work began on the building of the new church.

Father Spratt's record of activity in the teeming, poverty-stricken Dublin Liberties of the day is prodigious. He founded orphanages, homes for repentant prostitutes, hostels for the blind and night refuges for poor women. In 1856 he set up the Dublin Catholic Young Men's Society. He was active in the Society for the Prevention of Cruelty to Animals and served on the committee that was endeavouring to get a Catholic university for Dublin city. He was involved, too, in the temperance campaign initiated by Father Mathew.

Among Father Spratt's many outstanding qualities was his rare ability as an orator. While on a visit to Rome in 1835 he was invited by the Jesuits to preach at their famous church on the Corso Vittorio Emmanuele, the Gesu. His performance so impressed Pope Gregory XVI that he presented him with the remains of St Valentine.

St Valentine's body was removed from the cemetery of St Hippolytus on the Via Tiburtina and shipped to Ireland. It arrived at Whitefriar Street on 10 November 1836 and his shrine may be seen there today.

Father Spratt died in 1871. In Glasnevin Cemetery, Dublin, a granite memorial stands over his vault in the O'Connell Circle, appropriately adjacent to that of his great contemporary Daniel O'Connell, who gained Catholic Emancipation for Ireland and who died twenty-four years before him.

Tomb of Father Charles

Passionist church, Mount Argus, Dublin

On 11 December 1821 a baby boy, the fourth child in a family of ten, was born to a young couple, Joseph and Johanna Houben, in the small village of Munstergeleen in Dutch Limburg. There was nothing to indicate that when he was to die, 72 years later, it would be in distant Ireland, where he would be a revered and well loved Passionist priest with a remarkable reputation for successfully interceding for favours and some dramatic cures.

The boy was called Peter Andrew and throughout his boyhood was fond of spending every spare moment he had helping out in the parish church, making himself useful in the sanctuary or dressing the altar. In fact, the church seemed to be his second home. Although his school reports were usually poor, nevertheless the curé of his parish, Father Christian Delahaye, proclaimed: 'This boy will become great!'

Early in his life it seemed that his footsteps would one day lead him to the priesthood. This proved to be the case but not before he had served almost four years in the army.

The Passionist house at Mount Argus in Dublin, then on the outer fringe of the city, first opened its doors to Andrew Houben, now 'Father Charles', in July 1857. Almost a year after his arrival he wrote to his family in Belgium: 'There are five of us priests here, and five lay-brothers. In proportion to the great number of Catholics, there are in Ireland few priests, and every Sunday I have to say two Masses. Almost every day we hear Confessions from morning to night — if we had twelve priests every one of them would have much to do hearing Confessions and preaching. One can do much good here in the garden of the Lord. As you know, Ireland is a Catholic country, its population almost 8,000,000; and for more than 300 years

The tomb of Blessed Charles, Mount Argus, Dublin.

the Irish have suffered cruel persecutions, but in spite of all have remained true to the Catholic Faith'.

Over the years, Father Charles worked tirelessly at Mount Argus and his remarkable reputation for effecting cures grew. Early evidence of what was to come was contained in a letter written by another priest at Mount Argus to a friend about 1860: 'A boy of twelve years of age, who had lost the use of his legs, was brought to me by his mother and I made no delay in calling Father Charles to bless him. When he was engaged in blessing the child, I went to my room to change into my secular dress in order to go to Dublin. And great was my surprise when, on leaving the house, I found the boy walking about perfectly cured.'

The second testimony came the following year, recorded on oath: 'Father Charles was called to visit a neighbour of ours, called Thomas Doyle, who lived in 23 Lower Ormond Quay. Father Charles came and saw the sick man; but, when about to leave the house, surprised all the members of the family by saying: "But there is another sick person here!" No one had told him that a daughter of the sick man, Johanna Teresa, was also sick with a fever. They were not prepared to bring the visitor to her, as the room was not tidied up, and they tried to persuade him from going to see her. But Father Charles insisted ....

'(The girl) was ill with typhoid, or some other malignant fever, and was so exhausted that Dr Willis said that if she could not rest and take a little sleep she would die. She had not been able to sleep for several days. When Father Charles came, she was sitting up in bed, but in a delirium. The fever had reached its crisis and she had refused to take the prescribed remedies. Father Charles placed his hand gently upon her forehead and quietly pressed her backward until she was in a recumbent position. Almost immediately she began to sleep and when the doctor returned next morning the crisis was passed and he declared the patient to be out of danger.

'My mother frequently spoke to me about this event, and always said that she considered it as a miracle. She always declared emphatically that no one had spoken to Father Charles of the sick girl. I was also told that the doctor regarded the cure as miraculous; he was a Catholic. The girl in question was restored to health in the normal way and lived for many years afterwards.'

Countless accounts of cures attributed to him flooded in through the years that followed, until his name and reputation for sanctity became a legend in the Dublin of the declining Victorian era.

Father Charles of St Andrew died at Mount Argus on Thursday, 5 January 1893.

Tomb of Father John Sullivan

St Francis Xavier's Church, Upper Gardiner Street, Dublin

The Church of St Francis Xavier in Upper Gardiner Street in Dublin is perhaps the best known Jesuit church in Ireland. There, in its Sacred Heart Chapel, behind an ornate grille, a plain wooden coffin stands on trestles. It prompts a steady stream of worshippers to drop to their knees in prayer, for it is the last resting place of a local boy, a most unlikely Jesuit, a most unlikely candidate for sainthood.

Perhaps not as many pilgrims come to this shrine as are attracted to a similar place of devotion only a few city blocks away, the tomb of Matt Talbot, the saintly Dublin labourer, in the Church of Our Lady of Lourdes in Sean MacDermott Street. Yet, so many years after John Sullivan's death in 1933, more and more are finding their way to Gardiner Street to pray at his tomb.

By coincidence, the young John Sullivan was ordained at Milltown Park, the Jesuit theological study centre in south Dublin, on the same day, 28 July 1907, as the devoted and heroic Father Willie Doyle, also a Jesuit, who was killed at Frezzenberg in Belgium while ministering to wounded soldiers during the First World War.

John Sullivan was born in Dublin's fashionable Eccles Street, in Number 41, on 8 May 1861, a year when Dublin, then the 'second city' of the British empire, was honoured by one of its extremely rare visits by Queen Victoria, accompanied by her Consort, Prince Albert, just four months before his sudden death from typhoid fever.

The child's father was Edward Sullivan, Lord Chancellor of Ireland. Although born in Dublin, John had deeply rooted links with County Cork. His paternal grandfather had been a prominent wine merchant in the town of Mallow, while his mother was the daughter of a wealthy land agent with considerable property in the south of Ireland.

Tomb of Father John Sullivan

Born into wealth and position, of a mixed marriage, he was raised, together with his brothers, a Protestant, the religion of his father. This followed the custom prevalent at the time: if a couple's religions differed, girls of the marriage were raised in the religion of their mother while the boys were brought up in that of their father.

At the age of twelve, John was sent to Enniskillen, County Fermanagh, now in Northern Ireland, for the first stage of his education at Portora Royal School. When he was eighteen, he returned to Dublin, to enter the Law School of Trinity College. He was already in his thirties when he found himself attracted to his mother's religion and this eventually led to his reception into the Catholic Church. He was received in the famous Jesuit house in Farm Street, London on 21 December 1896.

Although, as a layman, he had become fervently religious, with much of his spare time being devoted to good works, it must have been something of a shock to his family and friends when, in 1900, he entered the priesthood. He began his studies at St Stanislaus College, Tullamore, County Offaly, a step that was to lead him, seven years on, to his ordination at Milltown Park.

John Sullivan's early years as a Jesuit were spent mostly on the teaching staff of his Order's prestigious college for boys, Clongowes Wood, in County Kildare, known as 'the Eton of Ireland', and at Rathfarnham Castle, Dublin, about the time the Jesuits were starting their well-known house of retreat for men there, which continued to flourish as such until the Order sold the property in 1985. During those years, his devotion to duty, his self-sacrifice and his unobtrusive sanctity had become well known.

Years later, his biographer, the well-known Jesuit writer Fergal McGrath, was to say of him: 'From the beginning of his life as a Catholic, John Sullivan seems to have felt himself to be called to the priesthood. There is no record of how the interior call came to him, but he spoke openly of his leanings to friends of his'. Among these were the constant visitors to his father's home in Eccles Street, family friends who included some of the most distinguished politicians and legal and literary figures of the day.

It was the opinion of several of those who knew John Sullivan well that he was first inclined towards becoming a Franciscan, because of his spiritual value of poverty. Certainly at that stage of his life he was a frequent caller at the Capuchin Friary in Dublin's Church Street, where he had several close friends in the community. It is believed that at one stage he was about to apply for admission to the Order's novitiate in Rochestown, County Cork.

John Sullivan's closing years were spent at Clongowes, which he had first known as a young man. Although he was on the teaching staff and had few contacts outside the college, it was during those years that his reputation for sanctity became widespread and swept through the people of the surrounding County Kildare countryside until it reached the proportions of legend in that largely farming and horse-breeding area.

A daily occurrence in his life from then on was the constant stream of people coming to see him, to ask his intercession for relief from countless ills. Frequent cures were claimed and were attributed to him.

On his death at the age of seventy-two, on Sunday, 19 February 1933, he was buried in the tiny community cemetery at Clongowes. For many years his grave, with its simple metal cross, was a place of pilgrimage. Later, as the cause for his canonisation gained momentum, his remains were removed to Dublin where, in the Jesuit church in Gardiner Street, a special shrine had been prepared.

Tomb of Matt Talbot

Church of Our Lady of Lourdes, Sean MacDermott Street, Dublin

Suddenly the man stumbled and fell to the ground, his slight, frail body crumpled in grotesque anonymity on the rough surface of Granby Lane at the rear of St Saviour's, the neo-Gothic Dominican church that had been built in the middle of the nineteenth century in Dublin's splendidly Georgian Dominick Street.

It was Trinity Sunday, 7 June 1925, the hottest day of a long heatwave, at a time of numerous and obstinate strikes in Ireland, when the Dublin Metropolitan Police had just merged with the Garda Siochana and the Dublin United Tramway Company had introduced motor buses on city routes. But all of that was irrelevant to the pathetic figure sprawled on the cobblestones of Granby Lane.

Matt Talbot, Dubliner, timberyard labourer, one-time layabout, one-time drunkard, hidden ascetic and a total abstainer from alcohol for many years, whose cause for canonisation would one day go to Rome itself, was dead.

In an early biography by Sir Joseph Glynn it was recorded:

'Far from showing any signs of the holiness which characterised his manhood and later life, he became somewhat addicted to drink, and spent his money in the public house instead of in his home. His mother, in after years, used to tell how he sometimes sold the boots off his feet for drink and came home in his stockings. This continued until he reached the age of twenty-five, when, one Saturday night, he suddenly announced to his mother his intention of taking the pledge. She was not very enthusiastic about this sudden resolution, but wished him "God speed" and the grace to keep it.

'He went to Clonliffe College, where he saw the Rev. Dr

The tomb of Venerable Matt Talbot, Sean MacDermott Street, Dublin

Keane, from whom he took the total abstinence pledge for three months, intending, as he afterwards told his mother, to break it when the time was up. At the end of the period, he renewed it for a year, and then for life. Eleven years later, Dr Keane congratulated him on being able to keep a total abstinence pledge, that being the time before Pioneers were heard of, and was delighted to hear that it was he who administered the pledge to this poor penitent. Matt related the story at home with great delight.'

That most distinguished Irish biographer Mary Purcell has researched deeply this period of Matt's life. In her biography of Talbot she quotes a sister of Matt's, Mrs Andrews, in recalling his taking the pledge:

'My mother said ''You're home early, Matt, and you're

sober!'' He replied ''Yes, mother, I am.'' After dinner he remained in the house, which was not usual, and finally he remarked to my mother: ''I'm going to take the pledge.'' She smiled and said: ''Go in God's name, but don't take it unless you are going to keep it.'' He said: ''I'll go, in God's name.'' As he was going out, mother said: ''God give you strength to keep it.''

'He went to Clonliffe, made his confession, and took the pledge for three months. He had been a couple of years away from the Sacraments then. Next morning — Sunday — he went to Holy Communion. On Monday he went to 5 a.m. Mass in Gardiner Street and was at his work as usual at 6 a.m. This he made a regular practice of from that on; but after his work, to keep away from his companions, he used to walk to a distant church, either St Joseph's, Berkeley Road, or St Peter's, Phibsboro, and remain there until bedtime.

'Once or twice — possibly on a Saturday — he went with the men to the public house, but he drank only minerals, and he usually spent Saturday afternoons away from where he might meet his old companions, and generally in a church. He had a bad time of it at first and sometimes said to my mother that, when the three months were up, he would drink again.'

Mary Purcell quotes another sister of Matt's, Mrs Fylan, on this crucial period of his life, those months following the day he took the pledge.

'He was a changed man immediately after taking the pledge. We never heard him swear again. He put two pins in the cuff of his coat to check any temptation to swear.... His workmates were astonished when they heard of Matt taking the pledge; and they were still more astonished when he kept it.'

Matt Talbot was born on 2 May 1856, in a small house, Number 13, Aldborough Court, off Dublin's working-class North Strand. The house was one of a row almost obliterated without trace by a landmine dropped from a

German aircraft on another May day eighty-five years later, during the 1939-45 war.

When Matt died in 1925 he was buried in Glasnevin cemetery on the feast of Corpus Christi, but in 1952 his body was exhumed and placed in a vault in the O'Connell Circle, one of a series of vaults surrounding that of Daniel O'Connell, the Liberator, the man credited with the winning of Catholic Emancipation in Ireland in 1829. The initial inquiry into Matt's life was opened in 1931 and in 1937 a Papal Decree introducing his cause was signed.

The remains of Matt Talbot were to be moved one more time. In February 1962 they were taken from the Glasnevin vault and placed in a tomb of Wicklow granite in the Church of Our Lady of Lourdes in Sean MacDermott Street, a Dublin church where Matt had frequently prayed.

There, through a glass panel, his coffin may be seen. Carved in the stark granite there is a simple inscription: *The Servant of God Matthew Talbot 1856-1925.*

Ballintubber Abbey

Thirteenth-century Augustinian foundation in County Mayo

It is chastening to realise that an abbey whose walls still rise, windswept yet unbowed, over a remote stretch of country in the west of Ireland, dates from the time of the Fifth Crusade, was a year old when Magna Carta was signed by King John at Runnymede in 1215, was 276 years old when Columbus discovered America, and had been in use for 350 years when Shakespeare was born. It is 300 years older than St Peter's in Rome and is contemporary with Notre Dame, Chartres and Santiago de Compostela.

This is Ballintubber Abbey on the shores of lovely Lough Carra at the end of a twisting road almost forty miles from Galway city, the only church in the world in which Mass has been celebrated for almost eight centuries. Among such abbeys it is unique in having been in continuous use for more than 750 years.

Ballintubber had royal beginnings. It was founded by Cathal O'Connor, King of Connacht, for the Canons Regular of St Augustine, and was three centuries old at the time of the Reformation.

Cathal O'Connor selected his site with respect for the past for it was at that spot, close to the beneficial waters of Lough Carra, that St Patrick founded a church in the fifth century.

The name itself enshrines the saint's memory, for Ballintubber comes from the Irish *Baile Tobair Phádraig*, or the Town of the Well of Patrick. Close by is the well where St Patrick baptised the first converts in the district, while twenty miles away to the west rears the saint's own holy mountain, Croagh Patrick, one of the oldest pilgrimage places in the world. Indeed, the abbey became a stopping place for pilgrims traversing what was called Tochar

Ballintubber Abbey, County Mayo

Phádraig, or Patrick's Causeway, on their way to the holy mountain that, as a place of pilgrimage, is more than 600 years older than the shrine of St Thomas à Becket at Canterbury.

The story of Ballintubber unfolded down the centuries. In papal taxation records of Pope Clement V, compiled in 1306, the goods of the House of the Fountain of St Patrick (Ballintubber Abbey), excluding their churches, were valued at £9.10.5 in the currency of the time. From 1400 several letters from Popes of the fifteenth century written to Ballintubber survive — from Boniface IX, Martin V, Pius II, Paul II and Callixtus III. During archaeological investigations in the 1960s the Papal seal of the letter of Pius II (1463) was unearthed.

The abbey was suppressed by King Henry VIII and, although it was stripped down to its bare walls, it continued to be used for divine service. In the year 1600 the Augustinian friars are recorded as having settled at Ballintubber.

Then came Cromwell, whose soldiers stormed the abbey in 1653 and ransacked and tried to burn the buildings. Although on that traumatic occasion the outer roof was destroyed by fire, the stone-vaulted internal roof of the chancel, four small side-chapels and the thirteenth-century sacristy escaped damage. The people, with that persistence which must be the keynote of Ballintubber's remarkable survival, continued to come there to worship.

Over the difficult years following the Cromwellian trauma, the abbey continued to be used. Because of the devotion of dedicated priests and a faithful people it was to function throughout the dangerous years of the Penal Laws, between 1690 and 1760.

The nineteenth century was to bring happier times. Almost as soon as the Act of Catholic Emancipation was passed in 1829 the people of County Mayo set about planning the restoration of their venerated abbey. By 1846 they had installed Gothic windows in the nave and transepts.

The inspiring last chapter of the Ballintubber restoration story was written in the 1960s. This final stage began in 1963 with a deep archaeological investigation of the site, followed by the careful restoration of the abbey church, which was completed in time for the celebrations that marked the 750th anniversary of the foundation of Ballintubber, held in 1966. At that time, the then Archbishop of Tuam, Archbishop Joseph Walsh, said:

'The most remarkable fact about Ballintubber is that from the time of its foundation up to the present day (except, perhaps, for a short period during the time of severest persecution) the holy sacrifice of the Mass has been celebrated without a break within its walls. Down through the centuries — even in the Penal Days — the people gathered at Mass in the abbey, having no roof but the dome of heaven.'

Croagh Patrick

The Reek, St Patrick's mountain, County Mayo

'Printer's ink will not give these wonderful hues; and the reader will make his picture at his leisure. That conical mountain to the left is Croagh Patrick: it is clothed in the most magnificent violet colour, and a couple of round clouds were exploding as it were from the summit, that part of them towards the sea lighted up with the most delicate gold and rose colour...'

Thus Croagh Patrick presented itself to a famous American literary man in 1842, no less a personage than William Makepeace Thackeray, just as, half a century earlier, a distinguished French visitor, Chevalier de la Tocnaye, had been greatly impressed by the large crowds of pilgrims he saw there, painfully making their barefoot way to its craggy and unsympathetic summit.

Nowhere do the Irish pay homage to their patron saint more fervently than at this mountain they call Croagh Patrick, or the Reek, towering 2,510 feet over the southern shore of Clew Bay. Just five miles away is the picturesque town of Westport, with its gracious Mall, flanked by lime trees, and familiar as the setting for several of the novels of George A. Birmingham (Canon Hannay) who was rector there.

The great day on Croagh Patrick comes each year on the last Sunday in July, known as 'Garland Sunday'. This latter dubbing has its roots in an old legend that tells us that a witch threw water over Patrick as part of a spell intended to kill him, but the saint swiftly turned the tables on her by hurling his bell at her and thus bringing her wicked activities to an abrupt close.

This bell of St Patrick, together with its elaborate shrine, may be seen in the National Museum in Dublin. It was used

Pilgrims on the rugged path on Croagh Patrick, County Mayo, with Clew Bay in the background and (below) the statue of St Patrick, with the mist-topped Reek in the background

during the closing ceremonies of the thirty-first International Eucharistic Congress in Dublin in 1932 and again during the visit of Pope John Paul in 1979.

Originally, the annual penitential climb to the summit of Croagh Patrick took place on St Patrick's Day, but as this falls on 17 March, the weather was usually too severe, so the pilgrimage was changed to July. Until the 1970s it was made during the hours of darkness but in the interest of safety it now takes place in daylight.

The ascent of Croagh Patrick, a steep mountain on every side, is usually made from Murrisk, where a small abbey, founded by the O'Malley clan for the Augustinian Friars, contains a beautiful five-light east window, together with the tomb of the founder of the O'Malley family.

Legend has it that it was on this mountain that St Patrick spent the entire Lent of the year 441 in prayer and fasting. In emulation, for countless years, pilgrims have scaled these painful slopes in their bare feet to reach the small plateau, about half an acre in extent, with panoramic views of island-dotted Clew Bay and all the jagged tracery of the western coastline.

Here, on days of pilgrimage, Mass is celebrated continuously in the open air, confessions are heard in the small St Patrick's Chapel and pilgrims follow the Stations of the Cross across the rugged stones.

The summit of Croagh Patrick on its south side ends abruptly in a steep precipice, and this spot is the traditional setting of the source of the legend which tells us that St Patrick rid Ireland of snakes and all venomous creatures. St Patrick stood on the cliff edge here, tradition has it, and rang his bell. As its knell re-echoed across the barren mountain top, a great swarm of adders, toads, lizards and many other venomous creatures came in countless numbers and flung themselves over the precipice!

Knock

Cnoc Mhuire — Mary's hill — Ireland's principal marian shrine, County Mayo

Fifteen people stood in silence that day in the remote village of Knock in County Mayo, gazing spellbound at the strange apparition that had appeared at the gable wall of their small parish church. The images lasted, clearly definable, for two hours.

It was 21 August 1879, a warm enough day at the end of summer, a workaday Thursday that should have been like any other but was, in time, to change the destiny of this unknown little village and make it Ireland's principal shrine and one of the world's greatest centres of devotion to Our Lady.

The apparition seen clearly against the weathered church wall consisted of three figures, Our Lady, St Joseph and St John the Evangelist. Our Lady, in white robes and wearing a golden crown, had her hands raised in prayer. On her right stood St Joseph and, on her left, St John, wearing a mitre and holding a book in one hand while the other seemed to be indicating an altar behind him on which a young lamb could be seen clearly.

The apparition at Knock was treated with every caution by the Church authorities, first by the parish priest of the time, Archdeacon Cavanagh, and later by the celebrated John McHale, Archbishop of Tuam. Within seven weeks, the Archbishop had set up an ecclesiastical commission before which the fifteen people who had witnessed the apparition gave evidence. All were considered trustworthy. When a second commission sat forty-seven years later, in 1936, there were only three survivors of the original group.

In the 1970s the then Parish Priest of Knock, Monsignor James Horan, had an incredible impact on the development

Pilgrims in procession at Knock

of the shrine. He built a large new church, which Pope John Paul II raised to the status of Basilica of Our Lady Queen of Ireland, and he was also instrumental, it is generally accepted, in persuading the Pope to visit Ireland and to attend the celebrations at Knock marking the centenary of the apparitions in 1979.

At Knock, Pope John Paul said: 'Here I am at the goal of my journey to Ireland: the Shrine of Our Lady at Knock. Since I first learnt of the centenary of this shrine, which is being celebrated this year, I have felt a strong desire to come here, the desire to make yet another pilgrimage to the shrine of the Mother of Christ, the Mother of the Church, the Queen of Peace.

' "Blessed are you among women, and blessed is the fruit of your womb!" This is also my greeting to Muire Máthair Dé, Mary the Mother of God, Queen of Ireland, at this shrine of Knock. Every time a pilgrim comes up to what was once an obscure bogside village in County Mayo, every time a man, woman or child comes up to the old church with the apparition gable, or to the new shrine of Mary, Queen of Ireland, it is to renew his or her faith in the salvation that comes through Jesus, who made us all children of God and heirs of the kingdom of heaven. By entrusting yourselves to Mary, you receive Christ!'

Monsignor Horan was also responsible for the existence of an international airport at Knock. The apparently outlandish project of constructing a major airport in the middle of a County Mayo bog, miles from anywhere, was greeted initially by amusement and scepticism. However, entirely because of Monsignor Horan's unceasing efforts, it became a reality and opened for business in 1986. Ironically, shortly afterwards, Monsignor Horan died suddenly in Lourdes.

The prescribed ceremonies for the pilgrim at Knock consist of making the Stations of the Cross, reciting the rosary and then walking in procession around the grounds of the basilica. The pilgrimage season opens on the last Sunday of April and closes on the last Sunday of October. The last Thursday of each month is observed as a special day for invalids.

Kylemore Abbey

Benedictine haven of the Twelve Bens

Few communities of nuns in Ireland have a home as picturesque, or one set in such magnificent surroundings, as the headquarters of the Benedictine Order, the Irish Dames of Ypres.

Set squat against a hilly background and lapped on its doorstep by one of the loveliest lakes in all Connemara, a few miles from Letterfrack, County Galway, Kylemore Abbey is a place of abiding tranquillity, one of those havens where the very silences are a prayer.

'We cannot imagine Kylemore without the nuns, although there are still a few folk around who remember the abbey before they came. It was called the Castle then', an old man told me on the road to Letterfrack.

The nuns are well established now at their lovely home at Kylemore, having been in residence there since shortly after the 1914-'18 war. They are an integral part of this lovely landscape that sprawls around the mountain range called the Twelve Bens. Yet, because of the girls' boarding school which they founded in the abbey, their fame — and the name of Kylemore — have spread far beyond the shores of Ireland and have prompted many foreign families to send their young daughters here for their education. The abbey must retain a special niche of its own in the memories of many grown women in many parts of the world who recall carefree schooldays in this gracious old mansion by the lake.

Kylemore Abbey, or Castle as it was called before the nuns came, is not an ancient house as large Irish country mansions go. It was built in the 1860s and just over twenty years later prompted the admiration of an energetic English writer, Alexander Innes Shand, who encountered its charms in the course of a long hiking holiday in the west of Ireland:

Kylemore Abbey in its sylvan setting in Connemara

'Anything more romantic it is difficult to imagine. To the right is the precipitous mountain, where the trees not only hang on somehow, but contrive to flourish luxuriantly among the huge boulders of grey rock and the blooming patches of purple heather; while to the left we soon look down upon the lower of the Kylemore loughs, the broad avenue being bordered by a magnificent fuchsia hedge in full flower.

'And before us, with its square towers and its battlements, seemingly buttressed by the precipices of the mountain behind, is the great Gothic edifice of Kylemore Castle. For superb views and commanding situation the site could not have been more happily chosen.'

Kylemore was built in the 1860s by a wealthy Liverpool merchant and MP, Mitchell Henry, who had fallen in love with the wild Connemara countryside during a holiday trip to the west. To design his dream home Henry called on the services of the distinguished architect of the time, James Franklin Fuller, who allowed his romantic imagination full flight. This resulted in the storybook castle the nuns occupy today. It is an imposing edifice of battlemented and machicolated turrets and slender towers, executed in fine local stone and seemingly rising up dramatically from the very waters of the lough.

'It is a splendid location for a girls' boarding school and

we are fortunate that the Sisters adopted this idea so many years ago,' a resident of Letterfrack said.

After Mitchell Henry's ownership, Kylemore was the Irish seat of the ninth Duke of Manchester during the early years of this century.

A small chapel stands some distance from the mansion itself, built by Henry, it was said, for his wife. Sadness overshadowed it from the beginning, caused by the untimely death of Mrs Henry.

The origin of Kylemore was remembered by Alexander Innes Shand:

'It was the choice of the late Canon Wilberforce who, after his conversion to the Church of Rome, settled down here in the wilds that he might labour for the good of the people.... Mr Henry, who, having fallen in love with the place, finally bought 13,000 acres of land from the Blakes of Renvyle. I need not say that since then he has been an enormous benefactor to the neighbourhood. The castle alone must have cost immense sums; and it was not only built but fitted up almost entirely by Irish workmen.'

Nor have the Sisters of Kylemore Abbey always kept their lovely and well-used headquarters to themselves. Apart from the countless young women who have enjoyed its ambience over an important phase of their lives, the general public have been welcome also, when, from time to time, the nuns have operated a restaurant in the fine old diningroom.

Even a disastrous fire some years ago did not daunt the good Dames of Ypres. They rapidly recovered from this stroke of ill-fortune to make Kylemore rise again, as solid and as lovely as ever, from its sparkling lake waters.

The church they dug from the sands

Monastic settlement of St Feichin, island of Omey, Connemara, County Galway

In the west of Ireland, on the island of Omey, off the Connemara coast, there is a tiny church that the people of this obstinate knob of land, unaided and with no sophisticated mechanics or drawing-board expertise, excavated from the sands. It was part of a monastic settlement founded in the seventh century by St Feichin.

While the preservationists may have viewed with some caution the exercise conducted without the advantage of any official advice or modern machinery, the more practical will doubtless have applauded the effort. The Omey site, if it had not been coaxed by timely local spades and shovels to yield its archaeological secrets, might well have been forgotten within another generation.

Over the centuries, since St Feichin first stepped ashore on Omey, the sands, driven by almost ceaseless Atlantic gales, had all but covered the extensive settlement he founded there. The top of one church gable-end still poked its way obstinately up out of the smothering sands, like the symbol of a religious faith that refused, down the centuries, to die, and it was this that tantalised the curiosity of the islanders.

When I first knew the island, it was a storybook paradise of utterly unspoilt natural charm.

'One of the most cheering aspects of what has happened on Omey,' a priest from an adjoining parish told me, 'is that it may encourage people in other parishes to take an active interest in such archaeological remains that may exist

The church they dug from the sands—before excavation (above) and after (below)

on their own doorsteps. Preservation, such as has been achieved here, can be effectively accomplished only at local level.'

Once a year, each August, Omey becomes relatively thickly populated as it fills up with neighbours from the mainland across the narrow neck of water, or visitors and tourists from further afield, on the occasion of its annual race meeting. This social outing hosted by the islanders is one of their most important days of the year, with pony and bicycle races held on Omey's firm sands and, sometimes, on calm days, currach (their traditional canvas boats) races held offshore, with punters and friends and strangers alike shouting their encouragement.

'The excavation of the church has created great interest,' a local man told me, 'and we've had more visitors than ever over the summers since the news spread. Even foreigners appear to be interested!'

Omey covers about 500 acres and it is a tradition of the island that when St Feichin first laid eyes on it in the seventh century and stepped ashore to found his monastic settlement, he discovered that it was the haven of the last pagans left in Ireland.

Before the great drain of the famines of the 1840s when Omey, in common with the mainland and other little islands close to it, like the rock-bound High Island, lonely Friar Island, Cruagh of the lonely shore and, to the south, the islands of Inisturk, Turbot and Eshal, filled the coffin ships with emigrants bound for America, there was a flourishing stocking manufacturing industry on Omey. The tradition of the island women's fine handiwork lingers on.

The excavation work on the little island continues, an abiding interest with the people of the little village of Claddaghduff, and such an ancient monastic site is likely to go on unveiling fresh treasures as the years pass.

Local people will tell you that when it was first decided to excavate around the tip of the gable wall that protruded from the sands, several official bodies were informed of the islanders' intentions. However, their readiness to listen to official advice was greeted with little more than indifference or, in at least one instance, complete silence. Consequently, on Omey the spades and shovels came out and the digging commenced.

It was slow, tedious and backbreaking work and, although there was little or no archaeological skill or ecclesiastical knowledge available, everybody was extremely careful that the excavations should be carried out with no damage or disturbance to the ancient building that was gleaming new when St Feichin prayed within its walls.

Slowly, sometimes agonisingly, the work continued, with the local men giving every minute of their spare time to it. Eventually, the sand had all been laboriously removed, the last boulder heaved aside and the ancient church fully revealed for all to see.

Of all the holy places of Ireland, few can be as quietly impressive as this 'lost and found' little church of Omey.

Sligo Abbey

Thirteenth-century Dominican friary at Sligo

Sligo Abbey is a Dominican friary founded in 1252 by Maurice Fitzgerald, Earl of Kildare, who was Justiciary of Ireland and who also built a castle on this site. Today it is in the heart of Yeats country, and the poet and Nobel prizewinner spent much time in the area and is buried in Drumcliffe.

The town and its friary came under attack many times down the years. The abbey was accidentally destroyed by fire in 1414, but was later restored by a friar named Brian, a son of Dermot MacDonogh, a chieftain of the area, although restoration work seems to have been confined to the church itself. After the sack of Sligo in 1641, the abbey lay in ruins.

Of this once great monastic settlement, its nave, choir and south transept still survive, with a tower at the junction of the three. The conventual buildings, in the usual format of Dominican foundations, lie to the north of the church.

The most notable features of Sligo Abbey are its eight thirteenth-century, deeply-splayed, pointed windows on the south side of the choir, its four-light east window, its groined roof beneath the tower, its magnificent arches and the pillars of the cloisters.

The abbey contains some interesting seventeenth-century monuments. One of these is the mural on the south wall of the choir, dating from 1623, to the local chieftain O'Connor Sligo, in which he is represented kneeling in prayer beside his wife. Another is the altar-tomb of the O'Creans in the nave. Dating from 1616, it has the names of Cormac O'Crean and his wife, formerly Johanna Ennis, carved on the bevelled edge of the mensa. There is a central depiction of the crucifixion with a flanking Virgin Mary and

Sligo Abbey cloisters

St John, along with St Dominic, St Peter, St Catherine, an Archbishop and St Michael.

Beneath the beautiful fifteenth-century east window of the abbey is a carved altar of nine panels, with an inscription and the date 1506.

The tower of Sligo Abbey has impressive lofty arches and

a groined roof. The cloister, on the north side of the nave, is almost intact on three sides, and may be especially remembered by the pilgrim for the magnificent workmanship of the arches and their coupled pillars.